positive
parenting
for a peaceful world

positive
parenting
for a peaceful world

a practical guide for the first twelve years

Ruth Tod

Foreword by Janet Bloomfield, Oxford Research Group

Gaia Books

A GAIA ORIGINAL

Books from Gaia celebrate the vision of Gaia, the
self-sustaining living Earth, and seek to help
readers live in greater personal and planetary harmony.

Editorial	Jonathan Hilton
Design	Lucy Guenot
Production	Louise Hall
Direction	Jo Godfrey Wood
	Patrick Nugent
Index	Kathie Gill

 ® This is a Registered Trade Mark of Gaia Books

ISBN 1-85675-236-4
EAN 9 781856 752367

This edition first published in 2005.
A catalogue record of this book is
available from the British Library.

Printed and bound in China

10 9 8 7 6 5 4 3 2 1

Contents

Foreword

I became involved in peace work in the early 1980s as an anti-nuclear activist. Marches, meetings and outrage were all part of my life. Outrage that my government was going to introduce US missiles into our country without the consent of the people. I was furious about it all . . . I was also the mother of two young children. One day a friend gave me a beautiful window sticker. It had a dove and a rainbow and said, "This is a peace house". Looking at it made me consider whether I could put it up in my window and feel that I truly did live in a "peace house". Was my family putting peace at its heart as much as we were active in CND? We thought it over and decided that we would put the window sticker up, but that for us it was not a badge of activism but an emblem of our commitment to try to live peacefully together. I really wish that we had had a copy of Ruth Tod's book then to help us!

In her introduction, Ruth writes, ". . . more and more people are questioning the morality and effectiveness of war as a means to bring peace. The need to use peace-making skills is more obvious than ever before, both at home and in the wider world". My experience as I travel the country as a speaker and trainer bears this out. Violence does not work, but neither does the denial that conflict is part of life. This book is a toolkit of wisdom, common sense and practical ideas that will guide people to a more skilful way of being in the world.

Its particular focus on peaceful parenting is very important. The moral panic about the behaviour of the young in our society that is stirred up by the media feeds on the aggression in words and behaviour that we see all around us. A book like this can help us stop and think about how we are bringing up our children and give us ideas and guidance that, if widely read and applied, have the potential to be deeply transformational. Its emphasis on the potential for fun and joy and loving relationships in family life is very refreshing in these cynical and controlling times. In an ideal world, the government would give all new parents a copy. I will certainly be giving it as a gift, to go along with the customary teddy bear, when anyone I know has their first baby!

I hope that all who read and use this book find themselves living in a true peace house . . .

Janet Bloomfield
June 15, 2005

Janet Bloomfield is the British Coordinator of the Atomic Mirror, a non-profit programme using the arts to raise awareness of nuclear issues. She was Chair of the Campaign for Nuclear Disarmament (CND) 1993–6 and currently serves as an honorary Vice-President. In Britain, she also serves as a senior consultant on UK Security Policy to the Oxford Research Group, and as a member of the Peace Campaigning and Networking Group of Quaker Peace and Social Witness. Internationally, she sits on the administrative council of Abolition 2000 – a global network of more than 2000 citizen groups working for a nuclear-free world. She writes and speaks widely on peace and disarmament issues in the UK and abroad, and is based in Saffron Walden, England.

> Creating a peaceable family is like a journey that starts whenever we decide to start it. It is a journey because we are always experimenting, testing, gaining new experiences, and changing.

1 Introduction

> ... peacemaking skills, such as empathizing, listening, consensus-building, and reconciliation, are needed both in our personal and political relationships.

The meaning of "peace"

When I was a child at home, I was fortunate to be part of a loving, nurturing family. We lived in a city in the north of England that was in the process of turning itself from a declining commercial centre into a vibrant metropolis. My mother loved caring for us, my father enjoyed his job, and we had a house to ourselves. The large garden surrounding it provided a sanctuary from the world.

To begin with I had no clear idea of what "peace" really meant. At school I was good at being polite and quiet, fitting in with others, avoiding outright disagreement, hiding upset or anger. Gangs and bullies were not the problem they are today, though some children seemed always to be quarrelling or fighting. I liked to stay out of trouble, so my friends and I kept well away. Until, that is, I was about ten years old and my sense of justice started to conflict with my under-standing of "peace", and I saw that peace had to include fairness and honesty. Being "quiet" was fine up to a point, but not when someone was being unfairly treated or a teacher had made a mistake. All my skills at being polite and accommodating had to be updated, because I was still determined to be a "good" girl. I began to discover that there was a middle way to be walked, a path between actually getting into a fight and keeping out of the way.

I also began to see justice and peace in a far wider context. In the school next to ours, I saw children who seemed to be very different from me. I have a strong memory of looking anxiously at their forlorn, pale faces and thin, undernourished bodies. I learned that they lived in overcrowded conditions and ate poor-quality food because their parents were unemployed. These children were unobtrusive and well behaved, at least on the streets. Perhaps they did not have the energy to be angry.

Changing the mindset

After this early experience, I was always troubled by pictures of suffering, of women and children, desperate and wounded by war or dying of malnutrition. This being the time of the Cold War, I had friends who were frightened of the Soviet Union. Many people believed that peace could be maintained only as the result of the threat of nuclear weapons lying in wait, serving as a deterrent to the other side. What sort of peace was this that depended on fear and created so much suffering?

Today we are still living in much the same mindset – we still fear what we do not understand and think that force, or the threat of force, will serve to hold "peace". Now more countries have the potential to use nuclear weapons and the death toll from wars all over the world continues to rise, as does the general level of fear.

It seems clearer than ever that peacemaking skills, such as empathizing, listening, consensus-building, and reconciliation, are needed both in our personal and political relationships. Here are some fundamental truths that apply in every context:

◊ Peace is never won through violence. Violence, bullying, and war breed more violence, anger, and war in a vicious circle of suffering.

◊ Peace cannot be won by ignoring violence, oppression, or injustice. Pretending all is well does not make the problem go away.

◊ Peace can only be won when all parties build bridges toward each other. This is as true of the family and the school as it is of neighbours, communities, and countries.

Fortunately, more and more people are questioning the morality and effectiveness of war as a means to bring peace. The need to use peace-making skills is more obvious than ever before, both at home and in the wider world.

HOW THIS BOOK IS ORGANIZED

The chapter headings reflect the essential qualities that can support us:

◊ To feel **comfortable** and confident in ourselves (Chapter 2).

◊ To **communicate** clearly and calmly (Chapter 3).

◊ To **care** for others and share with them (Chapter 4).

◊ To be **capable** of making good choices (Chapter 5).

◊ To **connect** what we do in the family with what we do in the world beyond (Chapter 6).

These qualities are important in all areas of our lives. When we value ourselves and care about others, we are able to create good relationships. When we are able to communicate our feelings and needs and to make connections, we are more likely to stay calm and caring in a conflict. We have the foundations for peaceable living.

Peace is not something just to be wheeled out in a crisis. Peace is for every day, and the more we practise peace the more we will be able to deal peaceably with conflicts when they arise.

What this book aims to give you

This book is a tool kit to help parents and carers work together with the children in their charge, to develop some skills and resources for living peaceably, not only with family and friends, but also in the world of school and later in work, neighbourhood, and beyond. Skills such as empathy, expression, sharing, consensus-building, and reconciliation are all building blocks for peace in many different situations. What we learn in the home is a resource for life that we can apply wherever we go.

Many of us have a rather woolly idea of what "peace" really is. So let's start by understanding it a little. Peace is not for those who want to live a quiet life! Peace demands energy, enthusiasm, and emotion! Peace involves active engagement with people – to be fought for peaceably.

This is not a recipe book. We cannot bottle peace and say "Apply this and all will be well". Nor can we capture it and hang a label around it saying "Please do not disturb". People who want to keep things "peaceful" all the time will find that they are chasing an impossible dream. They may be dispirited or disappointed. Or they may try to control everyone and everything by imposing their views and closing their minds to other possibilities. This imposed peace is not real peace.

This book is about active engagement with people and problems so that we are better able to understand one another and find solutions that value our differences and common needs. I will be using the word "peaceable" rather than "peaceful" because I wish to emphasize our ability to shape our lives. "Peaceable" means developing skills and abilities that enable and actively help us to make or create peace. In a peaceable family, everyone develops and practises these skills together, as equals.

Peace is:
◊ Respecting ourselves and others.
◊ Relating well to one another.
◊ Reconciling differences.

Responses to conflicts

When there is a problem, we usually deal with it in one of three ways: flight, fight, or turnaround. We try to ignore it. Or we start to argue and perhaps to fight. Or we take the peaceable route, which is to turn things around and look for a solution together.

FLIGHT

◊ FLIGHT may mean literally running away or simply ignoring things and turning away. At times, this may be the best thing to do, particularly in a situation that is potentially dangerous. However, it is not the recommended solution for most everyday problems we encounter.

FIGHT

◊ FIGHT back with words, fists, or weapons. This will most likely escalate the conflict and/or hurt the other person either emotionally or physically.

TURNAROUND

◊ TURNAROUND is to stay compassionate, calm, and confident and find a peaceable solution that everyone is happy with.

Turning conflict around

THE SPIRAL OF CONFLICT

The spiral of negative energy intensifies conflict so that we become more obsessed with, or more committed to, our ideas.

TURNAROUND

The spiral of positive energy opens up the conflict, so that we can find solutions. This spiral unwinds the conflict.

For many people, being peaceable requires a complete turnaround in their thinking. The starting point is that we are all different, that disagreements are inevitable, and yet we can still make peace.

The turnaround option requires energy, but of a different type to that of flight or fight. It may, for example, involve determination and courage. It may also mean listening to one another, welcoming different views, seeing different options, or making new decisions. The turnaround option means developing positive attitudes and communication skills, finding time for one another, and thinking creatively so that we can live peaceably with others, wherever we are. This book will help you and your family to develop the energy and skills to do this.

Turnaround starts with four simple ideas, as described opposite.

◊ Conflict can be good. It does not necessarily lead to violence. The challenge for a peacemaker is not to bury conflicts, but to deal with them constructively in order to stop them escalating.

◊ There will always be differences and disagreements, which may or may not develop into conflict. We all have our own experience and perspectives and sometimes they will be difficult to resolve – so arguments and quarrels will be inevitable at times.

◊ When we acknowledge and talk about our differences, we may all be enriched. We may find a new solution that everybody likes.

◊ Creating peace uses positive energy. The energy expended in war and violence is negative because it draws us into more and more violence, resentment, anger, fear, and hurt. The energy involved in making peace, by contrast, turns this around.

Peace is a path

Creating a peaceable family is like a journey that starts whenever we decide to start it. It is a journey because we are always experimenting, testing, gaining new experiences, and changing. In this book I will often use the word "we" to mean all of us – children, parents, and carers – because the ideas and skills I describe are useful for everyone to develop together. We can see the journey as a difficult and possibly unsettling one, or we can see it as an interesting and perhaps challenging one that we make together.

As with any journey, we need to acquire the skills, knowledge, and resources to travel. On this particular journey, peacemaking skills cannot be learned overnight. They take a lifetime. But in a family that is committed to peaceable living, everyone will be learning together and changes can take place quickly.

On this journey we travel together, learning from one another. Children will copy what they see and pick up intentions and emotions. What goes around, comes around; whatever parents expect will almost certainly happen. If parents believe that their children will be awkward brats or trying toddlers, there is a good chance those expectations will be realized. If they assume their children will be kind and caring, there is a good chance that, with some planning and empathy, they will indeed be kind and caring.

What goes around comes around – our expectations have a big influence on our children.

LOW EXPECTATIONS

People on this journey do not feel threatened by arguments because they see differences and difficulties as an opportunity to learn together. They will be able to acknowledge each other's feelings – including anger and frustration. They feel good about themselves and their relationships with one another. They also have a sense of reality, of what is possible and reasonable in this finite world in which we all need to live together.

Like any journey, we may sometimes feel that we are walking a tightrope where we are balancing conflicting needs, or we are on a seesaw where we bounce up and down. I like to think of peace as a path that is going uphill, sometimes easily and gently along a smooth, green track, and sometimes steeply between boulders. We pick our way looking for footholds, trying one possibility and then another, not knowing what will be the best choice. We may find that events and experiences lead us to take an unexpected route, but still we have a sense of where we are going.

> As with any journey, we need to acquire the skills, knowledge, and resources to travel. On this journey, peacemaking skills cannot be learned overnight . . . But in a family that is committed to peaceable living, everyone will be learning together and changes can take place quickly.

HIGH EXPECTATIONS

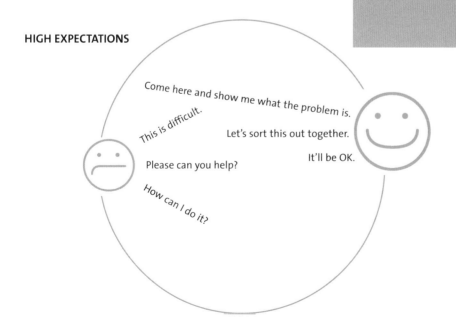

Come here and show me what the problem is.

This is difficult.

Let's sort this out together.

Please can you help?

It'll be OK.

How can I do it?

A tree grows outward from its core. So we, as individuals, take our values and skills out into the world as we grow.

Our roots are in love, empathy, compassion, honesty, and respect.

The peace tree

Creating a peaceable society is a little like growing a tree. The roots of the tree are our values, such as empathy, honesty, respect for ourselves and for others, and for the planet, while the branches are the actions and perspectives that grow from these. Like the concentric circles of the tree in cross-section, we grow outward from the centre, constantly developing the resources to live in a caring and constructive way. Family life is the starting point, the place where we learn our first skills and our core attitudes, which underpin and shape our responses as we move outward. The more we can help our children to acquire peaceable, practical, and positive skills, the more they can respond to life's challenges with confidence in themselves and consideration for others.

Creating a vision of a peaceable family

You can help yourself to create a peaceable family by having a clear, though flexible, picture of what it would look like. A clear vision of our expectations can help us to make it a reality because, in a subtle way, our expectations influence our responses and attitudes. If we are fearful that a child will be angry, then he almost certainly will be. If we expect him to be respectful, however, we are likely to teach and demonstrate respect.

One way to make your vision clear is to express it on paper, either in words or as pictures. If you can share this with your partner or the child's carer, even better. You, as individuals, may have different ideas about the details, but if you have overall agreement about your direction that will help you all.

TO CREATE YOUR OWN VISION

◊ Sit quietly with felt-tip pens and paper. Play some gentle music if you wish.

◊ Picture your ideal of a peaceable family. What are you all doing and feeling? Can you see them and hear them in your imagination. You may like to draw or write about this.

◊ What are the qualities that each person has? Are they comfortable, communicating, caring, and capable? Are they connecting?

◊ You may like to return to this exercise as you work through the book.

◊ Share your vision with other adults who are involved in caring for your child (grandparents, uncles and aunts, godparents, and so on). It will help you to understand and support one another.

> Peaceable parenting is not about taking control and having power over your children.

Not just a friend

Parenting is all about building relationships. If you find yourself feeling that life with your children has become a series of burdensome tasks, something has gone wrong. What you don't want is parenting to be a drudge or a battle.

So how do you avoid the battleground and bring joy into parenting? Peaceable parenting is not about taking control and having power over your children. Nor is it simply about being a friend to your children. It is about taking responsibility, about knowing when to exert your authority, about when to give your children choices, about how to support them in making decisions and behaving appropriately. It means being a friend – and also a carer, a model, a teacher, and an "awakener".

You may wish to be just a friend, but then it can be difficult to assert your authority or to give help, even when it is clearly needed. Children need their parents to provide security, boundaries, encouragement, example – and even advice. Before you read the rest of this book, take a moment to reflect on your role as a parent. This analysis can be applied to everyone who is involved in the care of children – extended family members and carers as well as to fathers and mothers.

A parent's role

◊ A parent as a friend brings love, equality, understanding, giving and receiving – and fun.

◊ A parent as a carer takes responsibility for their child's needs with love and attention.

◊ A parent as a model sets an example, which their child will copy.

◊ A parent as a teacher shows their child, helps them gain the skills and knowledge to learn and develop.

◊ A parent as an "awakener" listens, encourages, widens horizons, and stirs the imagination.

You may well find that you don't all agree about parenting because we all have our own particular gifts and views depending on individual experience of life. I hope the tools that I describe can help you share your ideas and reach agreement on the things that matter most to you.

Of course, the balance between the different roles parents have change over time. Can you visualize these different roles from your own experience? My own children are twins and when they were babies my main role was that of a carer, running around in small circles, struggling to understand and meet both their needs at the same time. Soon I also became a teacher, showing them how to do simple things. I was also keen for them to learn to care for each other and tried to do this by setting an example. I soon learned that this was not enough and that teaching, reminding, and requesting were all important, too.

> Peaceable parenting is about taking responsibility, about knowing when to exert your authority, about when to give your children choices, about how to support them in making decisions and behaving appropriately.

A friend brings love, equality, giving, and receiving

Are we having fun together?
Are we respecting one another?
Are we sharing?

A carer takes responsibility for a child's needs

Are you healthy?
Are you happy?
Are you getting a chance to do the things you enjoy?

A model sets an example

Am I staying centred in myself?
Am I setting an example to him?
Will he see in me the skills I most hope he will acquire?

A teacher teaches skills and knowledge

How can I help him to develop the skills he needs?
How can I help him to learn?
Am I helping him to understand?
What can I learn from him?

An "awakener" listens, encourages, and widens horizons

Am I noticing what he likes to do?
How can I encourage him to do the things he likes?
Am I open to understanding him?
What kind of person is he becoming?

Being comfortable
means that we
have a strong
sense of "self". We
feel at ease with
ourselves and
with others.

2 Being comfortable with yourself

> When we have a sense of self-worth we have the confidence to understand ourselves and others.

I'm OK; you're OK

Being comfortable with yourself is one of the most important keys to peaceable living. Being comfortable means that we have a strong sense of "self". We feel at ease with ourselves and with others. We have a growing sense of our own self-worth, self-awareness, and self-respect. This is an essential part of creating a peaceable life because, in difficult situations, we are less likely to be angry and more likely to stay cool, calm, and collected.

When we have a sense of self-worth we have the confidence to understand ourselves and others. We are able to negotiate with others because we have a sense of what we can tolerate; we know how to speak up and put our point of view across calmly and clearly. We also have the confidence to listen to others and to care about them and their views, no matter how different they are from ours. We appreciate our own viewpoint as well as theirs, so we are more able to find a solution that suits everyone. We meet one another and solve problems together as equals. We feel great, and so does everyone else.

A sense of self

It is a common mistake to think that having a sense of self-worth is the same as being selfish. When we behave selfishly we tend to generate controversy, to put the blame on others, to expect more than our fair share, to see things from our viewpoint only, and perhaps force others to do what we want. Another mistake is to think that instead of being selfish we have to be selfless. In this we give in to others and suppress our own views. But then we can feel resentful or useless, which, in turn, can generate ill feeling, possibly leading to an emotional outburst in the end anyway. Those with a weak sense of self are far more likely to feel threatened by differences because they do not have the skills and beliefs to help them deal with them constructively. So-called bullies are often like this.

Being comfortable and confident is neither selfish nor selfless. We can be assertive in difficult situations without being selfish, and we can be helpful to other people without being selfless.

A lifetime's learning

As parents and carers, one of our most important tasks is to support our child's sense of self-worth. In this section we look at some of the ways we can help each other to be comfortable and confident. The more we can do this, the more we can all cope constructively with conflict.

We can't learn this overnight; you could say it takes a lifetime. Babies start life with no awareness of themselves as separate beings; their first cries are mingled with the faces of those who care for them and their first movements catch objects around them accidentally. Toddlers love exploring their place in their world and the impact of their actions upon it. By four years of age, most children have a clear sense of themselves and of others as individuals.

> As parents and carers, one of our most important tasks is to support our child's sense of self-worth.

THE DIFFERENCE BETWEEN SELF-AWARENESS, SELFISHNESS, AND SELFLESSNESS

Selfishness

Blaming others.

Selflessness

Feeling a martyr or blaming others.

SELF-RESPECT
Affirming and affirmed
Confident and caring
Connected to others
Aware of oneself

Self-awareness

Able to stand back and notice.

Sharing and connected.

Caring and compassionate.

Secure and belonging.

Social skills.

Three sorts of love

To feel comfortable in ourselves we need to be loved and affirmed, to be appreciated and valued as we are. Then we can feel confident and relaxed about ourselves, reassured that we are complete and special human beings in our own right.

"Love" trips off the tongue so easily we can forget what the concept really means. It is an over-used word so often associated with romance, but there is no adequate alternative to convey the free flow of generosity and compassion that is love.

Love is not just kisses and cuddles; it is also being understood and acknowledged, given attention and consideration, given the space and the opportunity to become ourselves. In a loving environment we have

TOUGH LOVE gives little room for a child to think for herself and become herself because she has to obey without question. Either she will try to fit in with expectations and do what is forced on her, or she will resist and protest. If we look more closely, we can see that this is not parenting through love, but parenting through fear.

**TOUGH LOVE
(I know best)**

Follow these rules!

Go to your room!

Do as I say!

FREE LOVE, on the other hand, may be tempting, but it will mean that a child will have little sense of relating well to others because she learns only to please herself. This, also, is not really love because it avoids the type of responsibility and caring that are essential in a loving relationship. In an extreme case, a child may feel she can do anything that she likes, with no sense of the hurt and damage that she can do to herself or to others.

**FREE LOVE
(Do what you like)**

Take whatever you want!

Have a good time!

Don't bother me!

a role, we find a sense of purpose, we feel connected. We belong and feel secure.

In the following pages I will be exploring what it means to love and affirm and why this is crucial for peaceable living. Most parents and children love one another and want to be happy together. So what goes wrong? One of the reasons for things not working is that we sometimes have only a hazy idea of what it means to be loving.

In a peaceable family, love means appreciation and affirmation combined with clear expectations and examples of how to behave. This is a supportive kind of love that helps each person to be herself and relate well to others.

> In a peaceable family, love means appreciation and affirmation combined with clear expectations and examples of how to behave.

SUPPORTIVE LOVE
(Let's work this out together)

Yes, what a good idea.

Please can you help me do this?

How lovely, thank you.

No you cannot do this because it is not safe.

SUPPORTIVE LOVE is set within a clear framework of expectations and boundaries that encourages caring and consideration for oneself and others. Supportive love is the basis of peaceable parenting because it teaches us to deal with problems from a constructive, caring position. It is not imposed. It is taught through affirmation and appreciation, example and explanation, with clear limits as appropriate. It is a practice that is constantly developing and two-way. As we affirm and appreciate our children and ourselves, they feel affirmed and they, in turn, learn to affirm us.

The power of affirmation

Some people find the idea of affirmation difficult because they think it means blanket approval of everything someone does and says. They imagine that it will make a child over-confident, or "cocky". So let's be clear what it is and what it is not.

Affirmation means that you "walk alongside" your child. While criticism and punishment pull people apart, affirmation and appreciation bring them together to empathize and connect.

PUNISHMENT DIVIDES

Punishment and criticism pull people apart.

What a nuisance you are!

Go upstairs at once!

AFFIRMATION UNITES

Let's sort this out together!

Affirmation and appreciation bring people together.

Thank you, that's great!

Affirmation is:

◊ Supporting and encouraging what seems best and right and discouraging what is inappropriate or wrong.

◊ Appreciating a child as she is, without necessarily approving of her actions.

◊ Meeting her needs when you can.

◊ Showing and teaching her how to become a responsible, caring person.

The most precious gift you can give your new baby is your presence, your time, and your attention.

Love and affirmation is a journey that starts with birth, when a child is first welcomed into the world. The most precious gifts you can give your new baby is your presence, your time, and your attention. Welcome your baby into your lives as much as you can. Aim to put aside some of the other demands on your energy, because those first few months are uniquely precious.

WELCOMING ALL YOUR CHILDREN

Comforting

Having fun

Understanding her cries

Holding and hugging

Talking and listening

Resting

A welcome ceremony for a new baby is a key moment in many cultures, whether it is a church christening or a temple blessing. If you do not belong to a formal faith group, you might consider creating your own celebration. A party or a meal can give your friends and family a chance to bring gifts and perhaps to express their hopes for the baby and yourselves. Or you can create your own ceremony with poetry or music and symbols of hope and love, such as candles.

Family and friends can be a great source of support. My own family lived four hours away, so I used to take our children to them for extended visits. We were fortunate to live near my husband's family and to have good neighbours, who became extra grandparents. Together, their practical support and loving friendship was a huge source of strength.

Sibling rivalry

If you are worried about sibling rivalry, remember that it's important to give every child some of your time and attention. You can also show them how to love the new baby and involve them in her care. Sibling rivalry is probably inevitable at some stage. However, you will be able to keep this to a minimum if you continue this pattern of affirmation and caring for one another.

One way you may be able to reduce sibling rivalry is to encourage each child in the things they enjoy. Once they have had a chance to excel in what they particularly enjoy, children are usually willing and able to fit in with others, whereas children who are never given that chance are more likely to feel jealous of siblings. This may seem hard work when several siblings are clamouring for your attention, but it is important and worth it!

When they were about four, our twins wanted to do different things and would both demand attention. Affirming what they both enjoyed doing became a priority. Our daughter loved roller-skating and cycling, while our son loved ball games, so one solution was to take them both to the park; one to cycle and the other to practise cricket or football. Fortunately, the park was flat with plenty of grass and paths.

Supporting and affirming ourselves

The peaceable family is for everyone. It won't work if parents feel unappreciated, exhausted, and unsupported. When we are tired, it is easy to be cross and it can be difficult to keep a sense of proportion. So somehow we need to affirm ourselves, find time for ourselves, and get support when we feel we need it.

Affirmation is also important because it teaches us how to behave well toward each other. Children copy what they see and hear. They pick up attitudes and values just as easily as they pick up mannerisms. This means that you cannot teach them affirmation properly unless you affirm yourself as well as others. If you put yourself down or neglect yourself, your feelings will leak out and show somewhere else. Affirmation will help you feel better and it will help your children learn to affirm themselves and others.

> You cannot teach affirmation properly unless you affirm yourself as well as others.

Affirming yourself is quite a challenge when you are faced with many competing demands – a crying baby, a whining toddler, piles of washing, spilled milk – it may feel as if things are getting out of control. Just at that moment, self-affirmation is probably what you most need. It may be that you have to forget the washing and the milk and just sit down and hug your children. Of course, this may not be easy, especially if you long to sort everything out immediately, but if you can take a step back you may find that things go more smoothly afterwards.

Just for you
If you can't think what to do for yourself, a choices chart might help you generate ideas. This is what you can do.

Put yourself in the middle and write questions around the outside.

ACTIVE CHOICES

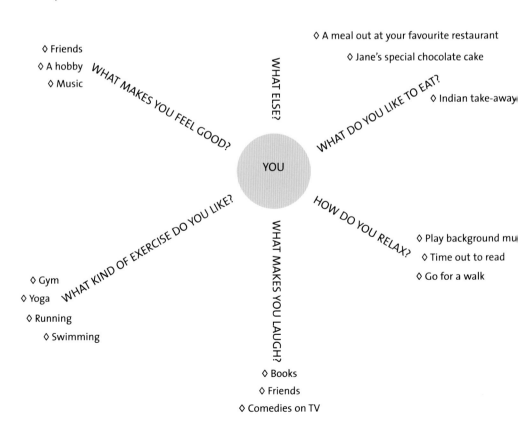

◊ A meal out at your favourite restaurant

◊ Jane's special chocolate cake

WHAT DO YOU LIKE TO EAT?

◊ Indian take-away

◊ Friends
◊ A hobby
◊ Music

WHAT MAKES YOU FEEL GOOD?

WHAT ELSE?

YOU

WHAT KIND OF EXERCISE DO YOU LIKE?

HOW DO YOU RELAX?

◊ Play background mu
◊ Time out to read
◊ Go for a walk

◊ Gym
◊ Yoga
◊ Running
◊ Swimming

WHAT MAKES YOU LAUGH?

◊ Books
◊ Friends
◊ Comedies on TV

WHAT YOU CAN DO TO AFFIRM YOURSELF
Prepare for your day
Take at least 5 minutes every morning to care for yourself – have a bath or a quiet time – do some simple stretches and welcome the day – massage your feet – breathe deeply and gently.

Visualize something you know you will be doing that day, even if it is something small, such as making a cup of tea for yourself. Having things, even small things, to look forward to is very important. Visualize enjoying it and doing it well . . . feel, see, and hear it going well in your mind's eye. This will help you to feel good about your day – make plans to help it go well. What do you need to do to prepare for it?

During the day, be realistic about your time and energy
PLAN – make a programme of what you hope to do – can you realistically do it all? What can you ditch? Avoid getting into a downward spiral of doing too much for others.

PRIORITIZE – write down what you most need to do, including giving yourself and your children some quality time. Can someone else look after the children to give you a break? If you are going to work, can you have fun at lunch time?

FIND SUPPORT – make time for people you enjoy seeing and who give you support. A group with similar attitudes and time for one another is reassuring and encouraging. It's also good to share childcare with people whom you trust and like.

REFLECT – what do you most enjoy doing and is there a way to do it at some point during the week? Do you need to find time to be together with your partner? Or do you need to see your friends? If it's difficult to get out, can you have some fun evenings in? Is there something you want to do just for yourself? Maybe you would like to watch a film you have been meaning to see or get a takeaway meal as a treat rather than as a necessity.

At the end of the day
KEEP the good things in mind – remember there is no such thing as failure; only feedback and learning. Learn to go forward.

RELAX and have fun with your family so that you can all unwind – listen to one another, tell stories, sing songs, read books, watch a favourite old film.

> Remember there is no such thing as failure; only feedback and learning.

Arguments and disagreements

Arguing over what we need and want and long for is one of the most common causes of disagreement and argument in families. As parents and carers we often feel bombarded with requests and demands. New shoes, new bikes, more sweets, an expensive toy, more computer games, another dog, another TV, a new breakfast cereal!

BEING BOMBARDED

Can I have some new shoes please?

Why can't I have those sweets now?

I need a mobile phone.

Why can't I have a computer?

Please, please could I have a TV in my room?

It's not fair! I want that game!

Everyone else has got a DVD player.

I want a bike like Tom.

Sometimes it is tempting to give in to children's demands, but of course we cannot and should not do this all the time. If we constantly give a child whatever she asks for, we give her a false view of the world and her own place in it. One of the best things we can do as parents is to understand which of all these demands are real needs and which are passing fancies.

Needs are important. When we fail to recognize our child's real needs, we are neglecting her or belittling her. She will respond either by arguing and fighting or by acquiescing and feeling ignored. However, when we help her to have her needs met we are valuing her and taking her seriously. We are also helping her to value and respect herself.

Of course, understanding our needs can be particularly hard. Can you recall times when you have been confused or uncertain about what you – or someone close to you – really needed? Perhaps you felt uneasy about something, but could not put your finger on why. Or perhaps someone was giving you lots of well meant advice that seemed inappropriate.

> When we fail to recognize our child's real needs, we are neglecting her or belittling her.

Needs, wants, and aspirations

Seeing the difference between needs, wants, and aspirations can help us to understand ourselves and one another better, and in this way avoid unnecessary argument and frustration.

    By **"needs"** I mean physical requirements for food, drink, warmth, and shelter, as well as emotional needs for love, respect, security, and freedom, and for a sense of purpose and connection. In Western society today, we are usually able to meet most of our children's physical needs. Emotional needs are just as important, but they are more complex. For example, we all need love and respect. As we have seen already in this section, love is not just a quick hug or a smile. Loving someone means giving our attention, our support, and our understanding. We also need to feel we belong to a group, although some of us like to be alone more than others. Some of us find a sense of purpose in supporting people or in leading them. Others like to get on with projects on their own. In one way or another, our lives need to have meaning.

    By **"aspirations"** I mean something we aspire or long to do – perhaps to perform, to climb, to paint, to sing, to cook, to grow vegetables – whatever it is that really awakens and inspires us.

    By **"wants"** I mean requests for things we do not actually need. As we have already seen, some requests or demands are exactly what your child needs right now, while some are mere passing fancies and are unimportant. For all that, however, they can give you a clue to what a child does need. For example, a demand for new shoes may be a physical need because the old ones are too small, but it may equally be a passing whim. Alternatively, it may reflect an emotional need to feel part of a group.

BEING CLEAR ABOUT WHAT NEEDS ARE
Needs are basic things, which include:
◊ food and drink
◊ warmth and shelter
◊ love and respect
◊ belonging and security
◊ a sense of purpose and connection

Understanding needs, wants, and aspirations is important because if we confuse them:
◊ We may not see what our child really needs.
◊ She may feel dissatisfied, misunderstood, or angry.
◊ We may have unnecessary arguments.

Sorting out needs, wants, and aspirations

Sorting needs, wants, and aspirations is like putting them all through a strainer. All the requests we are bombarded with fall into the bowl. As we reflect on and sort them, the wants and aspirations stay in the bowl, while the needs are shaken out, to be addressed.

Requests

Computer games
Magazines
Jeans
Pocket money
Sweets
New bike
New shoes
Bags
Footballs

More pocket money
New shoes
A new bike for your birthday

Real needs

Separating needs from wants

◊ Listen to what everyone is saying and you will probably hear each child saying what they would like – a bag, a football, a bike, a new computer game, a magazine . . .

◊ Ask yourself what the message is behind the words? How is the child expressing herself, what is she feeling and doing? Does she really need a new bag or does she need you to spend time with her, talking about clothes or going out together somewhere enjoyable? Or does she want her own football because it's not much fun playing with the boys? Perhaps your son's sport's kit bag is worn out. Perhaps it looks old fashioned and he feels awkward with his friends. If so, don't dismiss it lightly – take the opportunity to talk about it.

◊ Reflect on what may lie behind the wants and needs and you may detect some clues regarding aspirations – perhaps both your son and your daughter want to be footballers. Who knows? Ask yourself: "Am I discounting my daughter's aspiration to become a footballer? Am I failing to appreciate her properly?"

Does this mean we can never have treats?

This does not mean that we can never have what just takes our fancy. Having fun, relaxing, and celebrating are all important. Treats are good for us. In fact, we need them. It is important to remember that sorting out needs and wants is not a tool to control or pass judgement; it is a technique that can help us to understand our child better.

THE ICEBERG EFFECT

Please can
I have a new
pair of shoes?

Requests

This diagram shows us how we
can look beneath the surface
of a "request" to understand
it and then to explore the
possible solutions.

Are her existing
shoes too small?
Are they worn out?

Does she want
them because her
friends have them?

Underlying need

Shall we buy some new shoes?

Shall we talk about her friends?

Possible solutions

YOUR CHILD HAS ASKED FOR NEW SHOES

First of all ask yourself: "What is the message behind the request?"
Are they too small or worn out? If so, the need is obvious.

Suppose the shoes are still in good repair
◊ Is the request a passing fancy or is it a clue to a less-obvious
underlying need?

◊ Is this about belonging to a group? If so, you can take the
opportunity to ask yourself questions about this group.

◊ Do you feel that the group is a good place for your child to be?

◊ Would she feel left out of the group if she did not have
the shoes?

◊ If you bought the shoes, would you feel that you had given in
to pressures you don't like?

◊ If this is a habit, where might it end? Are you going to have to
buy more and more things so that she is happy in this group?

Once you have found some answers, you will be half way to
deciding what to do. It may be that she really feels comfortable
with the group and that this is an opportunity for you to meet
them and their parents to talk about a whole raft of things. Or it
may be that she (or you) is not too happy with this group and
that it is time to find another one.

THINGS TO THINK ABOUT

◊ We can't possibly say "Yes" to everything that a child asks for. Sometimes we can't provide it. Sometimes we shouldn't!

◊ When our real needs and aspirations are met we feel appreciated, supported, and comfortable with ourselves. When our needs are not met, we can feel upset, forgotten, or angry, so it is important to acknowledge them and explain why you cannot meet them.

◊ A passing fancy or an obsession may be a clue to an underlying need or aspiration that we are ignoring.

◊ Treats are good, too.

◊ At heart, we all have the same basic needs – we just meet them in different ways because we are all different people.

Social pressures

Understandably peer pressure may be a major reason why a child wants a new bag or clothes. The desire to look good and to have the "right" possessions are not just problems for children. Advertising encourages us all – adults as well as children – to want more, buy more and do more, while TV, the internet, and films open up a huge opportunity to experiment, to push out boundaries, and to take risks.

One way to manage this type of pressure is to talk about priorities and to set an example yourself. If you love shopping, for instance, it will hardly be surprising if your daughter does, too! You might find it helpful to connect to a group of like-minded people who feel the same as you. Their support and friendship can help you to create a norm that you are happy with.

Remember that there are limits to money and what it can buy. Loving, laughing, listening, and learning together are some of our real needs. Money can help us to do these things . . . but in the end we have to create things for ourselves! Our families need our attention and our time as well as our money.

Our own needs or our child's needs?

It is all too easy to think we know best about what our child needs, whether it's piano or karate lessons, more friends, or time on her own. Perhaps we have unmet aspirations of our own that we long to see our child taking up in our place. Perhaps we have fixed ideas about a safe and secure future. These may or may not be what she needs. To avoid this, it is important to give ourselves the time and space to notice and listen to her. One way to do this is to notice and encourage what she is curious about. What makes her happy, content, absorbed? She may not be able to do all those things, but she must have the opportunity to do some of them. It is also important to notice what troubles her. What worries her, limits her, or frightens her? What does she need that she is not receiving?

Because we are all different, the things we enjoy, the ways we react, and the skills we have are going to be different. When we notice how our children respond and how they feel, we can understand them as unique human beings.

> Because we are all different, the things we enjoy, the ways we react, and the skills we have are going to be different.

NEEDS

Don't confuse our needs with those of our children
Our gifts are the things we enjoy and are drawn to. When we see our children's gifts, we can see what their needs and aspirations are.

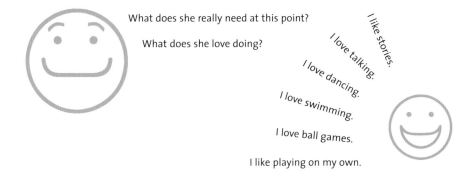

What does she really need at this point?

What does she love doing?

I like stories.

I love talking.

I love dancing.

I love swimming.

I love ball games.

I like playing on my own.

Conflicting needs

We can't always have what we would like. This is one of the hardest lessons to learn, especially for toddlers. As babies, they were cared for and their needs were satisfied as far as was possible. But now they discover that in reality there are other people in the world who have other ideas about what to do. Children who grow up getting whatever they want will have a hard time when they come to mix with others and discover that other people have different ideas that conflict with their own.

To help us deal with needs and demands we may be able to prioritize them or to balance them. To prioritize needs means acknowledging what is most important and what can wait. To balance needs means finding a way that keeps each person satisfied at the same time.

In the scenarios here (below and opposite), which solution seems right for you? But note that there is no "right" answer.

1. Each day you come back from work tired and hungry. Your children are well looked after by a carer, but now they need to be all over you.

What do you do?

Do you prioritize?
◊ Ignore your own needs and suffer in silence.
◊ Put your own needs first, so that you can meet your children's needs soon after.

Or do you find a way to balance all your needs together?
◊ Ask the carer to stay half an hour longer to make you a cup of tea.
◊ Prepare in advance by postponing your arrival and having a cup of tea in your favourite café on the way home.
◊ Figure out a way to make the journey home relaxing.

2. Your new baby cries a lot and your toddler is becoming more demanding. Both seem to need you equally.

What do you do?

Do you prioritize?
◊ Try to put the toddler first so when the baby cries you leave her until you cannot stand it any longer.
◊ Pay full attention to the cause and deal with it as best you can.
◊ Tell your toddler to go away and play.

Or do you try to balance the needs of both children?
◊ Give your toddler a doll of her own to care for.
◊ Involve her in caring for the baby.
◊ If this happens frequently, can you spend time with supportive friends who can help you?

3. Your partner complains that you spend too much time with the children.

What do you do?

◊ Ignore his needs and tell him he has to wait till they are older.
◊ Recognize his needs.
◊ Organize a babysitter so that you can go out regularly somewhere that you both enjoy.
◊ Involve him in the fun parts of childcare.

REMEMBER
◊ When we prioritize needs, we discover what matters most. We may find that we can meet all needs in turn, or we may find that some of them just fade away.
◊ When we balance needs, we may find a solution that suits us all.

THE BATTLE OF WILLS
Understanding needs, wants, and aspirations will help you to deal peaceably and positively with the battle of wills that is so typical of a toddler's behaviour. As we have seen, meeting our child's needs does not mean giving her everything she asks for or doing everything for her. It may be an easy option in the short term, but if she thinks she can have everything she asks for, she will be forever dissatisfied, because she will always be expecting more. The desire for instant gratification is unrealistic in the long term.

Facing up to a battle of wills is an opportunity to show:
◊ What is important and what is not.
◊ That other people have needs as well as ourselves.
◊ That some things can wait and some things cannot.
◊ That we are still loved.
The best time to start is with a toddler who is just discovering that she is not the centre of the universe. This is really important because it can be a key moment when we learn to give and take in life – although, of course, it is never too late to learn.

To help you teach about give and take:
◊ Meet your child's real needs *and* your own, if you can.
◊ Show her and teach her to see other people's needs *and* her own.
◊ Balance or prioritize needs so you find a way forward that affirms all concerned.
◊ Be generous – don't refuse her everything just because you are trying to teach her a lesson.
◊ If you make a promise to do something later, remember to do it.

> Peaceable discipline provides support and guidance, so that everyone has an idea of what is expected of them, what will be discouraged or not tolerated, and what will be appreciated and respected.

Affirmation and discipline

Affirmation is also the key to peaceable discipline because it helps us deal with conflicts relatively constructively. We have seen that affirmation helps children to be comfortable and confident in themselves. Affirmation involves loving and welcoming our children into our lives. It means paying attention to them as individuals so that their needs are met as far as possible. It means helping them to develop a sense of self-worth so that they can handle difference and conflict.

The idea of discipline tends to put people off because it is associated with harshness and rigidity and is based on punishment and judgement. However, there is a softer kind of discipline that provides support and guidance, so that everyone has an idea of what is expected of them, what will be discouraged or not tolerated, and what will be appreciated and respected. This kind of discipline is good for parents and carers as well as for children because it gives us all a framework. As with discipleship, discipline involves recognizing our own responsibilities and commitment to a way of life.

Affirmative discipline

Affirmation works because it creates a positive, self-reinforcing cycle. It draws people toward us, engages them with us, demonstrates empathy, and connects us to one another. Criticism and punishment may have their place, but when these methods are used frequently or inappropriately they are likely to create fear, anger, or resentment, which exacerbate conflict. They pull people away from us, break connections, and set us apart.

> As with discipleship, discipline involves recognizing our own responsibilities and commitment to a way of life.

Affirmative discipline accepts that anger is inevitable; it gives us the space we need to express difficult emotions and to deal with them constructively. It is flexible and forgiving. It encourages us to behave peaceably and responsibly because we care. Differences are welcomed as choices and opportunities. Mistakes are seen as an opportunity for learning, not for condemnation. Can you think back to times when you were punished and other times when you were affirmed? How did you respond?

CYCLE OF CRITICISM AND PUNISHMENT

I'm stopping your pocket money!

You naughty child!

Go to your room!

Feeds on itself and
pushes people apart.

TOOLS FOR CREATING THE POSITIVE CYCLE

Affirmation and appreciation create a positive cycle by reinforcing the attitudes and behaviour you wish to foster. They can bring out the best in all of us and help us feel good about ourselves. Here are some ideas to help you do this:

Appreciation means giving attention to the things you wish to encourage. When we say to someone something like "I loved the way you arranged those flowers", not only are they likely to continue to do that type of thing, but they will also feel good about helping and pleasing others.

When we are not happy with what a child is doing, the affirmative way is to redirect her to something more appropriate. If she draws on the walls of the living room and you don't want her to, it is important to say "No!" very firmly so that your view is completely clear. Follow it with a positive statement such as "I like this room as it is, please help me keep it that way". Then offer her an alternative – perhaps to draw on the walls of her own room or on flip chart paper that she can fix to the walls when she has finished.

Saying "No!" is essential when you really mean it and you can convey it in your tone of voice and body language. "No!" is for when you are in a hurry or in danger, when the arguments are getting nowhere and you need to move on, or when your children are just trying it on or are winding you up. Try saying a soft, low, firm "No!" – not too often, though, as its impact will wear thin.

Praise is complicated. When we constantly praise a child, we build up an expectation that they should always be good, but even children are human! It's not possible to be good all the time, so it's better to focus on appreciation to encourage their development and enjoyment rather than their success. Avoid saying "What a good girl, how clever you are". Focus more on the quality of what she has done by saying "What a cheerful drawing!", "Thank you so much for emptying the dishwasher", "You're really getting the hang of this now", "I love hearing you sing that song".

Constant praise soon loses its value and stops being noticed, so don't overdo it. Be specific and use your praise when you are really pleased or are keen to encourage a particular response.

CYCLE OF ENCOURAGEMENT AND AFFIRMATION

I'm sorry.

Thank you.

Please help me.

Draws people
together and creates
good relationships.

CLEAR BOUNDARIES AND MESSAGES

One of the keys to successful affirmation is to give your children a sense of belonging and security, appropriate for their age and nature. This means setting clear boundaries. As they become more mature and responsible, these boundaries will move outward and the rules will change – but they need to remain clear. One way to develop clear boundaries in your family is to create a set of family rules (see pp. 50–1).

USE WITH CAUTION!

Criticism, rewards, and punishments may create a negative cycle of resentment and argument, and so need to be kept in check.

Criticism is appropriate and necessary at times. The trick is to distinguish between the action and the person who did it. If a child accidentally runs into the road, it is obvious that you have to stop her and tell her she must never do this, in ways that are appropriate for her age. But if you tell her she is naughty or stupid, you are teaching her that she is no good. You are in effect disempowering her, when you need to be enabling her.

Rewards are great for real achievements. When we have worked at something special, it is good to be rewarded with a present or certificate. But rewards for small, everyday things become a type of bribe, and you may find you get cooperation only if you use them all the time. In addition, regular rewards sow the idea that if you are good you will always be rewarded, which is clearly untrue. Real life is just not that simple.

Punishment is always a negative action, though a child who is keen to please may appear to respond positively to it. When we are really desperate it may be the only thing to do. But if punishment becomes a habit, it builds up a negative cycle of resentment, anger, defiance, or fear. That is, if it seems to be effective. If you find yourself punishing a child, ask yourself what is she learning here and is this the best way to teach it?

If you often use punishment that does not work, it might help to think about what is going on. It may be that from your child's point of view it isn't a punishment at all – perhaps it is a convoluted way of getting your attention. In which case, it's worth thinking about giving her attention of a more creative, caring sort. Punishment and reward both have an underlying focus on obedience. Used as a habit, they are a tool for controlling a child rather than supporting or teaching her.

Security and freedom

To feel comfortable with ourselves we need to feel secure. But we also need the chance to push out beyond the comfort zone and do new things. This tension between security and freedom is one of the most common causes of conflict. On the one hand we need to give our children security and on the other we need to trust them to go out and explore. This is one of the most important gifts we can give our children because it enables them to meet the world less with fear and more with confidence. It means that they are more open and less defensive; more able to understand, negotiate, and reconcile differences between people.

On the one hand we need to give our children security and on the other we need to trust them to go out and explore.

Why security is important

When we feel comfortable and secure in ourselves we are more able to deal with the unknown, physically and emotionally. The more confident we are in ourselves, the more we can offer friendship or understanding to those with a different attitude or way of life.

Feeling safe comes first. The baby that is carried and hugged is likely to feel safer than the baby who is left to cry until it is time to be fed or changed. Meeting her needs when she cries brings affirmation and security. Her cries are the first signs of an individual who can shape her own life, even if she has no idea of that, as yet. When comfort and a sense of safety come, she receives love and the beginnings of confidence in herself.

Why freedom is important

Yet our concern for safety must be balanced by a willingness to trust. The toddler taking her first steps will be unsteady and sit down with a bump of delight on her padded bottom. Fond, onlooking parents can only marvel at her ability to let go as the ground slips beneath her. Smile with her and she will pick herself up and continue; look anxious and she may be less sure of herself and hesitate to start again. The same applies to older children who fall over and hurt them-selves. If we flinch and seem worried, they will almost certainly mirror us and start to cry. If we give them encouragement and perhaps a quick hug, they are more likely to pick themselves up and move on.

> Growing up is all about the balance between freedom and protection, responsibility and support, risk and safety.

Finding a balance

To feel comfortable, children do not need to be wrapped in cotton wool. They need the kind of security that gives them the support to explore, so that they can feel confident in their abilities and at the same time know their limits. Growing up is all about the balance between freedom and protection, responsibility and support, risk and safety. The art of peaceable parenting is to respond positively to this constantly changing balance, to know when to let our children take risks and experiment and when to say "Not yet!" In this uncertain world, we cannot protect our children endlessly from what might happen. Rather, we need to give them the resources to know what they can do, what risks to take, and how they can prepare.

**SECURITY AND
FREEDOM/BALANCE**

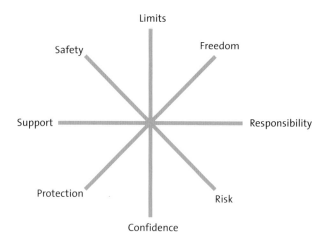

Expandable boundaries

To juggle this delicate, flexible balance, it is important to have clear boundaries that our children can test. I don't mean there should be rules that are constantly being broken and argued about. When the goal posts keep moving arbitrarily we feel confused and frustrated – and loads of energy gets wasted in arguments. When we have a clear sense of what is expected and what is possible, then we can feel safe and supported. Even so we may feel trapped.

Part of the process of growing up is about pushing out those boundaries, of testing them and negotiating new ones. Life is an adventure in which risk-taking stretches us and teaches us. So it is really important that the boundaries should be flexible, growing outward and being life-enhancing. All through life we need to learn how to extend ourselves so that we grow to feel confident in new capabilities. This is a continuing process; one that needs to start in our childhood.

Boundaries need constant reassessment as the family group changes. If one parent goes away for even a few days, he or she may be surprised to see that new skills have been learned or new experiences assimilated. Children are learning all the time. Sometimes we refuse to move the boundaries because we simply do not see or anticipate these changes. All that then happens is that we hold our children back and prevent them from moving forward. Sometimes it is more convenient for us if our children stay the same. Perhaps we find it difficult to adjust to change in them. For example, we may prefer to keep them in a pushchair rather than let them walk because it is hard to slow down and give them time to explore.

> All through life we need to learn how to extend ourselves so that we grow to feel confident in new capabilities.

> Creating family rules can be an excellent way to resolve differences between parents because your views are out in the open and you can see that you have different assumptions and expectations.

Family rules

One way to create flexible boundaries is to agree on family rules. These can be useful as they help everyone know where they stand. Without rules, parents may disagree and so children can leap in and play one off against the other. Or parents may argue between themselves about what they think is best.

Creating family rules can be an excellent way to resolve differences between parents because your views are out in the open and you can see that you have different assumptions and expectations. You may not reach agreement about everything, but at least you will know where you are, and that will be fine, provided you agree over the essentials. In fact, by acknowledging minor differences you teach your child that difference is all right and that people have differing views that can be listened to and discussed.

You can start to create family rules as early as you like. By the time a child is four years old, she is probably old enough to discuss rules with you.

CREATING YOUR OWN FAMILY RULES

When you make your rules, I think there are probably five principles to bear in mind:

1. You need to create the rules together – parents with the children and carers, as appropriate. Everyone needs to be involved in setting the rules because this will help to create a joint sense of commitment to keep them. You will need to be open about the differences so that you can reach a compromise or consensus.

2. Family rules provide both boundaries and expectations, so it's important to make them positive and constructive.

3. Some family rules need to be fixed and non-negotiable, because they are concerned with safety and/or moral values.

4. Other family rules can be flexible, depending on the situation and who is in charge. These rules are a guide to help everyone respect and support one another.

5. Family rules change as children become more responsible. What works at one stage may not work later, so you need to be ready to move on.

FIXED FAMILY RULES
For example:
◊ Keep away from fire.
◊ Cook only when an adult is present.
◊ Stop, look, and listen before you cross the road.
◊ Cross the road only at the traffic lights or zebra crossing.

FLEXIBLE FAMILY RULES
For example:
◊ Bathtime at the weekend is at 7.30.
◊ Bathtime during the week is 7.00.
◊ Teatime is usually 6.00.
◊ Everyone has their own cupboard for their special things.
◊ The jobs rota is changed on Fridays.

REMEMBER
It is all right for people to have different approaches. Children who are given very fixed family rules will be frightened of flexibility. My children quickly accepted that at Grandma's we always had to take our shoes off and wash our hands as soon as we came into the house. But we did that in our own home only when we were grubby.

To create your own rules you might like to read the rest of this book first and then ask yourself:

◊ What matters most to us (safety, manners, responsibility, generosity, caring, tidiness, and so on)?
◊ What is realistic to expect from our children?
◊ Where can we be flexible and where will we be fixed (see above)?
◊ How can we best discuss changes to the family rules?
◊ How do we help our family keep to them?
◊ What can we agree to differ on?

A peaceable family
is one in which
we learn good
communication
skills, so they
become a habit
for all occasions.

3 Communicating with one another

Communication skills for peacemakers

Good communication skills are an essential part of peacemaking because they help us deal constructively with differences of opinion and disagreements. As I explained in the introduction, difference is an intrinsic part of being human. This is because we all – children and adults alike – have our own, unique perspectives and experiences.

Most of us tend to gravitate toward people who think much like we do because we feel affirmed and more comfortable in their company. However, difference is inevitable and to be welcomed. We have to deal with it.

When we are open and comfortable with ourselves differences can be exciting, rewarding, and broadening. But when we are closed, uncertain, or worried, differences are likely to seem threatening. We may feel inadequate or even fearful.

Many conflicts develop because we are frightened in some way or because we do not have the skills to deal with the conflict constructively. Further conflicts develop because we tend to assume that others think like we do. Our intention may have been good, but we simply forgot to consider other people's views or feelings. This section explains some ideas and tools that we can use to help us.

THE ELEPHANT AND THE BLINDFOLDED PEOPLE

Five people were blindfolded and introduced to a baby elephant. One felt his trunk, another bent down to touch his feet, another patted his legs, another discovered his tail, and the fifth person was lifted onto his broad back.

When they described the elephant to one another, they started to argue. They had each discovered something completely different!

◊ It's like a snake with a strong, sucking tongue.
◊ It's soft and grainy, like a sack.
◊ It's hard and smooth, like a large shell.
◊ It's a whip, with a mind of its own.
◊ It sways and heaves.

In reality, of course, they were each correct because they had each discovered a different aspect of the same animal – the elephant. But because their experience was limited, their individual truth was incomplete. However, together they had an idea of the whole.

I think there is an important message here for all of us. It can be so easy to think we know it all or that our picture of something is right. The joy of the elephant story is that if we can learn from others and accept their truths, we can together find a better understanding or a better way forward. When we are open, we have so much to learn from one another.

Making a habit of communicating

Disagreements turn into conflicts when people do not, or cannot, understand each other. Either they are not listening or they do not have the ability to be calm and clear. If you think back to an argument where you were angry, can you remember what happened? Sometimes I jump to conclusions without checking the background or I misunderstand what someone said. This is easy to do and may well not matter. The important thing is to be able to retrieve the situation, to notice what is happening, and to sort it out before you get into a complicated tangle. Other conflicts are more convoluted, but they require the same skills of listening and explaining.

A peaceable family is one in which we learn good communication skills, so they become a habit for all occasions. We talk and listen as a matter of course. We have fun together and share our feelings. We argue and get angry, but we also resolve differences and find good solutions. All this takes time, but it is time well spent. We get to know one another: what we love, what worries us, how we see things, how we learn. The more we "bank" good times together, the easier it will be to bring up difficult subjects when we need to. We will be more open to hearing whatever our child says, whether it is pain or joy, imagination or fact.

Good communication involves listening and noticing as well as talking. It also involves most of our senses and our actions. We can see this in small children, where every moment of their expression is a delight to us. Small children respond to touch and feelings, to images, sounds, and smells. They notice the tone and volume of our voices before they know the meaning of the words we use. They respond to smiles and frowns, cuddles and laughter, anger and distress. They pick up tensions, however much we try to suppress them. We encourage them by listening and watching, playing back to them what they have said, laughing and smiling with them, affirming and hugging them. As children grow up, it is good to keep alive this whole spectrum of expression, to go on hugging and laughing and also to encourage expression through play, music, dance, or art.

> Good communication skills are an essential part of peacemaking because they help us deal constructively with differences of opinion and disagreements.

GOOD TIMES TO TALK

◊ Walking to school
◊ Tea time
◊ After tea
◊ Bedtime
◊ Reading
◊ Watching TV
◊ Drawing or any activity that you enjoy

Talking together can be fun, but if one person dominates the conversation, it rarely is. If you never seem to find the time to talk together, it might help to build "talking times" into your day.

It is important to encourage everyone to talk and to listen, because when we can express ourselves in words it is easier to be clear and constructive. Having the words to express ourselves can make all the difference between storm and calm. Words are tools that help us articulate our views, feelings, needs, and beliefs.

> Having the words to express ourselves can make all the difference between storm and calm.

If you feel there is something you need to know, try to avoid a barrage of focused questions, which may sound like interrogation. To encourage a child to talk, you can ask soft, open questions such as "What are you feeling?", "How would you like things to be?", "What can we do about it?", "What stops us doing this?" In the next few pages you will find some more detailed ideas to help you.

TALKING WITH A CHILD

What can we do about it?

What stops us doing this?

How would you like things to be?

What are you feeling?

I'm feeling worried.

My teachers says my writing is untidy.

I'll show you.

TIPS TO ENCOURAGE LISTENING

◊ Choose a time, such as after dinner, when you all take turns to talk about the day.

◊ You could give each person (adults and children) a few minutes to talk and when they have finished affirm them and perhaps ask questions.

◊ You could do this with each child on their own, if it is more appropriate.

◊ Or just listen. Sometimes a child simply needs to talk and all they need are a few nods and smiles of encouragement. There may be very little to say at the time.

Listening is as important as talking. People tend to talk about themselves a lot these days without always listening or taking an interest in what the other person has to say to them. For various reasons, people are becoming more and more self-involved. It is important to develop an exchange rather than just putting our own view across. When we listen we are giving our full attention, not interrupting with put-downs or criticisms, but affirming, perhaps with nods and smiles of encouragement. Children who talk easily are children who know what it means to be listened to and heard.

WHAT TO AVOID

Most of us know from experience what stops us sharing our thoughts and our feelings.

Here is a checklist of what to avoid if you can:

◊ Put-downs
◊ Personal criticism
◊ Ignoring people
◊ Complaints
◊ Teasing
◊ Sharp rebukes

◊ One of our greatest needs is to be understood and so one of the most precious gifts we can give each other is the gift of understanding and sharing.

◊ The more we communicate with one another, the more we create understanding of one another, so the easier it is to deal with difference.

◊ Communication becomes an intrinsic part of a shared life.

◊ The most important thing you can do is to keep lines of communication open.

Noticing is an essential part of listening because body language and tone of voice can tell us so much. When we hunch our shoulders, stare at the ground, and keep silent we are still communicating. When we shout angrily, burst into tears or thump the table, our words may be unintelligible, but we are certainly expressing some of our feelings.

Non-verbal communication may express our feelings more accurately than words, which can often be ambiguous. The other day my next door neighbour's toddler was playing with shells on the path and she started to stand on them. Before I knew it, I had said "No!" very firmly and she had burst into tears. A quick hug made things better in a way that my apologies and explanations would never have done. After that we could look at the broken shells and think about what had happened to them without judgement.

NOTICING

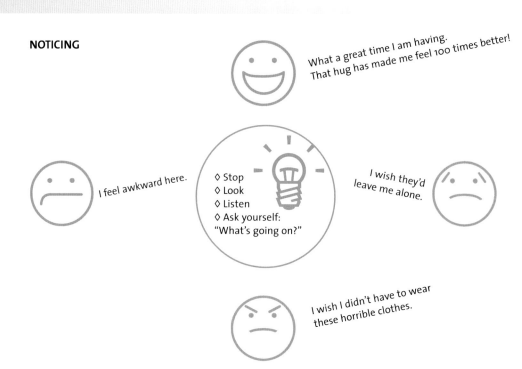

FAMILY MEETING AGENDA

◊ Washing up rota
◊ Where shall we go on Saturday?
◊ What shall we buy for Jim?
◊ Who will look after the neighbour's cat next week?
◊ The houseplants are looking a bit sickly – what shall we do about them?

Family discussions

One way to encourage good communication is to make time for family discussions. They can be a great way to nip problems in the bud, stop bad situations escalating, and resolve problems constructively.

You can do this quite lightly and informally. Talking round the table after a meal may be the best time, because you are already a gathered group and don't have to create a special situation or call a formal meeting. Sitting at a table can be good because you are all fairly close, so eye contact is easy. A round table is ideal because then there is no hierarchy and everyone is more likely to feel on an equal footing. The table itself provides a holding framework, although a circle of chairs and sofas could work as well. If everyone has enjoyed the food you will all be feeling relaxed. Perhaps you are still finishing the meal.

In our family, we had informal discussions over lunch at the weekend. If anyone was in a hurry, we would have to get talking straight away. Meals, in general, were good times to share what we were doing and planning and to catch up on family news, because it meant that we could be sure everyone had heard everything.

Some families like to have a regular family discussion at an agreed time, with an agenda that everyone has contributed to. You can have a list up on the wall for everyone to jot down items as they think of them during the week. These can be different kinds of things: what to do about jobs agreed to but not done, what to do about cleaning muddy boots or watering plants, where to go at the weekend, who to invite for tea, and colour suggestions for the dining room walls. Sometimes the agenda might include sharing feelings about a more complicated decision, such as moving house or about a mutual sadness.

Expressing feelings

Some people find it very hard, or even frightening, to deal with their feelings, whether they are joyful, positive feelings or angry, negative ones. Yet it is important to express them if we can because they give us vital energy to change and create. Feelings are a bit like a

volcano. Some of us bury them deep down so they get forgotten, or we might let them rumble and simmer underneath for days, until we explode with resentment or frustration. Others burst out with their feelings without any hesitation, which is usually fine when they are joyful, but unsettling or even threatening when they are angry. To help create a peaceable way of life, it is good to find a more flowing way to express our feelings, still pouring out of the volcano, but with a more creative kind of energy.

Learning to do this is not easy for most of us. Perhaps we find it difficult to acknowledge our feelings, even to ourselves – let alone to others. Perhaps we are shy or embarrassed, upset or angry. More often it is the case that we simply do not have the skills to communicate our feelings calmly and constructively. We cannot imagine how our feelings might flow out freely from the heart of the volcano.

> Feelings are a bit like a volcano. Some of us bury them deep down so they get forgotten, or we might let them rumble and simmer underneath for days, until we explode with resentment or frustration.

"I" statements

One of the best ways to communicate our feelings is to say simply "This is what I feel . . .". It is a very firm, clear way of communicating, because nobody can dispute it. Have you ever said to somebody "I feel sad" and then received the reply "No you don't"? I hope you haven't.

Whenever we make an "I" statement, first of all we say what we see or hear, then what we feel, and then what we need.

"I" statements are good because everyone – adults and children alike – speaks from their own point of view. Often when we are irritated with someone we get straight into an argument because we don't say how it is for us. Perhaps someone is refusing to help you cook dinner. What do you do? Do you shout at him or do you walk away in a temper? Instead, you might say "We need dinner and I am feeling very tired right now. I feel upset because you are not helping me." He might well be astonished by what you said, because he hadn't seen there was a problem up until that point.

"I" statements are good in a discussion or argument because each person gets a chance to be heard in turn, and in this way everyone gets to hear each other's feelings and needs. The facts, feelings, and proposals are separated out. Nobody says what they imagine anyone else is noticing, feeling, or thinking. Instead, they say what they themselves are feeling and thinking from their own experience and needs. The value of "I" statements is that each person learns to take responsibility for themselves and their feelings. They are a great way to stop ourselves from blaming and threatening.

Learning to use "I" statements

Using "I" statements is easy with just a little practice. Start by trying this technique for yourself. In this way you can learn how to use it and sow seeds that your children might copy. Notice your own responses as well as theirs.

"I see" . . . What are the facts?

"I feel" . . . What do I feel?

"I think" . . . What do I need?

REMEMBER
Focus on what you see and feel, not on what you think others feel, or ought to feel. Then offer a realistic solution.

TEACHING "I" STATEMENTS

I don't want to go.

It's not fair.

I hate her!

I can see you're angry and upset.

Please can you tell me why you feel like this?

What can we do about it?

I'd love to go.

I'm so excited!

She's great!

I'm so pleased you're happy about this.

Let's get everything ready.

"I" STATEMENTS IN ACTION

Here are some examples of how you can use "I" statements to express any feelings – your sadness or your pleasure:

"When you leave your toys in the garden, I am worried that the rain will spoil them and you will be upset. Let's bring them in together."

"When you leave your clothes in heaps on your floor, I feel upset because they look uncared for. I don't want to iron them again. So I'd like us to see how we can tidy your clothes."

"When your friends come round after school, I am really pleased that they come and say hello to me. I love to meet them."

In this next example you can see what can happen when Jill uses this technique with an older son, Jack. Notice the three stages. It may look slow and boring, but that is because I have written it out in detail. Once you get the hang of it, this technique can become second nature and very fast and effective.

JILL
Facts: Bedtime has slipped. We agreed you would go upstairs at 8:00 pm. Last night you did not go up till 8:30.
Feelings: I am worried that you are not getting enough sleep.

JACK
Facts: It only slips sometimes. Last night was an exception. Anyway I never get to sleep until about 9:00.
Feelings: I feel you are treating me like a baby. I don't feel tired.

What might happen next? You might argue about whether Jack is tired. Or you might agree to a trial period where Jack gets ready for bed at 8:00 pm and then does something quietly in his room from 8:30 to 9:00 pm, if he wishes.

SUMMARY

Each person speaks in turn. (Make sure that if you do this frequently you also take it in turns to start.)

◊ **Notice . . .** Say what you see. Try to be objective and specific, so that you are clear.

◊ **Feel . . .** Say what you feel and why. For example, you are upset, worried.

◊ **Propose . . .** Say what you want to happen next.

Play back

A good way to help children deal with their anger is to encourage them to say how they feel. The play-back technique may help. To do this, you simply notice and listen to them and then play back what you see and hear about their feelings. Before long they will start to talk about their feelings themselves. For example, Jenny has been using the computer for some time. Alice wants to have a turn and is very cross that Jenny won't let her. Both of them are now talking loudly. Here are some options:

◊ Tell them to stop and listen.
◊ You could say "It seems to me that Alice is feeling fed up because Jenny won't let her have a turn on the computer".
◊ Alice might say "It's not fair" and Jenny might say "I've got homework to do".
◊ Stick with feelings and say "I can see that you are both upset".
◊ Once they have both been "heard", they may be able to calm down.

Dealing with anger and arguments

I want it! It's mine! Give it back! It's my turn! It's not fair! When we are arguing, we usually go over and over the same ground, often without really listening to the other people. The challenge for peaceable families is not to bury arguments but to deal with them constructively.

Anger itself is not wrong. What is important is that we help one another to express our anger so that it does not lead to violence or other kinds of hurt. Usually, anger is an expression of an unmet need. Perhaps we feel ignored or misunderstood. Maybe we are frustrated because we cannot achieve what we want. Perhaps we are hurt because someone has put us down or maybe we are cross because we have to do something we do not want to do. Somewhere there is a need that is not being met.

For some people, anger may become a habit, a regular way of dealing with problems. When this happens anger can escalate into violence. If we are constantly getting cross, our children will mirror our behaviour and will become cross as well. However, if we respond calmly and constructively, they may copy that behaviour instead.

> Anger itself is not wrong. What is important is that we help one another to express our anger so that it does not lead to violence or other kinds of hurt.

MIRRORING BEHAVIOUR
Angry behaviour is copied

That man is dreadful. He makes me mad!

I'm really fed up with you!

You're a real nuisance!

That girl is a real pain. She makes me mad!

I hate you!

It's not fair!

Compassionate behaviour is copied, too

I'm so sorry. What can you do to mend it?

What a good idea! I wonder when we can try it out.

How lovely. Thank you.

Oh dear! Can I help fix it?

Please can we do this?

Thank you.

Children who know from experience that you will care for them in this way are less likely to be really angry.

Cooling anger: building a bridge

When someone is cross there are four steps you can take to help sort things out. Once you have taken the first two steps, you will be in calmer water and more able to work things out. In a crisis you will need to do this fast and cut corners.

1. **Calm** down or cool off. You could start by taking some deep breaths or count to 10 slowly. Turn down the TV or the music so that things are quieter. Ask everyone to stand still or sit down. With young children you could make a kind of game of this, in which everyone stands as still as a statue – and then relaxes. Some people send children to their rooms to cool down, but unless you are clear that this is the very best thing, it is likely to be interpreted as a punishment. This postpones or avoids finding a solution.

2. **Connect** to the other person or people. Make eye contact if you can and put your hand on them. Perhaps you can get everyone holding hands. Tell them you hear they are angry.

3. **Communicate** the facts as you see them, the feelings you have and the needs you have identified. Ask each person to do the same. Listen to each child in turn and encourage them to use "I" statements or similar (see pp. 62–3).

4. **Create** a solution together. Connecting and communicating builds a link, a bridge that helps us to empathize and connect with one another and to see things from different points of view, as described below.

Creating solutions together

There are many techniques for creating solutions. You may be able to combine everyone's ideas into something that is new and different, or you may need to work out a compromise that pleases everyone equally, if not entirely. Children who know from experience that you will care for them in this way are less likely to be really angry. The more you are trusted to understand and respect them, the more at ease they will be when something goes wrong.

To create solutions together you need to get the facts straight, understand one another's feelings, and meet everyone's needs – as best as you can. Sometimes a child is too uncertain or fearful to talk about their needs, so you need all your skills at watching and listening, without rushing in or judging. Their anger over something at home may have its origins in something bigger elsewhere, such as unexpressed worries about school.

One way to look for a solution in an argument is to use the idea of the iceberg. What you see and hear are the angry words and actions at the tip of an iceberg, with all the feelings and needs concealed beneath it. You can work down through the layers, first by identifying what people are saying and doing, then by identifying their feelings, and then by identifying their needs. Having done that, you will find it easier to find a solution that addresses the problem.

> To create solutions together you need to get the facts straight, understand one another's feelings, and meet everyone's needs – as best as you can.

THE FEELINGS AND NEEDS BENEATH THE FACTS

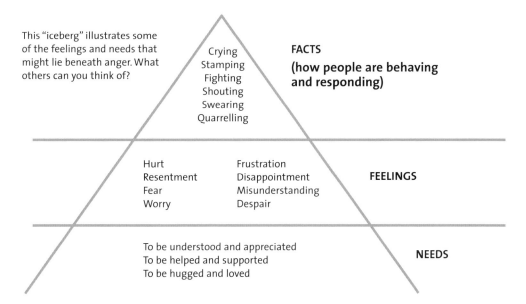

This "iceberg" illustrates some of the feelings and needs that might lie beneath anger. What others can you think of?

Crying
Stamping
Fighting
Shouting
Swearing
Quarrelling

FACTS
(how people are behaving and responding)

Hurt   Frustration
Resentment   Disappointment   **FEELINGS**
Fear   Misunderstanding
Worry   Despair

To be understood and appreciated
To be helped and supported   **NEEDS**
To be hugged and loved

AN EXAMPLE

Suppose two children are quarrelling over the same toy or game. Do you take it away from them and tell them to play together "nicely" or to play on their own? If you were to do this regularly they would soon learn the lesson that they temporarily lose the things they argue over.

Or do you use this as an opportunity to teach them something about cooperation and sharing? If so:

◊ Get the facts clear and watch what is happening.
Is this the only game of its type available for the children to use? Is one child getting more turns than the other?
◊ Notice how they are feeling. Are they both angry?
Or is one child angry while the other is pleased and cocky?
◊ Identify what you think they need.
Do they really want to share comfortably?
Or do they need to have a quiet time on their own?
Or do they need to have your attention for a while?

Agree solutions based on their needs and feelings. If they really want to play together can they take turns or create a game that allows them both to share? If they need time apart, can you help them to do something different? If they would like to do something with you, have you got time right now, or later? If it is going to be later, say when it's going to be and then keep your promise – or at least offer to, otherwise that strategy might not work next time.

RESOLVING DISPUTES

This model is useful for disputes in all situations. Older children and adults may be able to do this without a guide, though in difficult situations a facilitator can help.

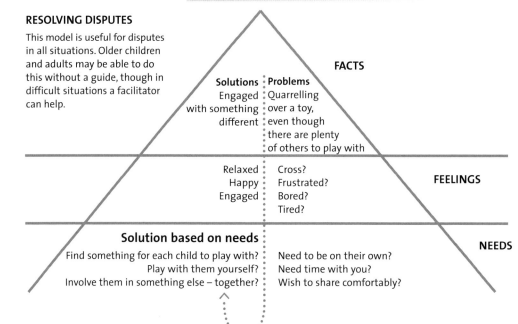

FACTS

Solutions : Problems
Engaged : Quarrelling
with something : over a toy,
different : even though
: there are plenty
: of others to play with

Relaxed : Cross?
Happy : Frustrated?   **FEELINGS**
Engaged : Bored?
: Tired?

Solution based on needs
Find something for each child to play with? : Need to be on their own?   **NEEDS**
Play with them yourself? : Need time with you?
Involve them in something else – together? : Wish to share comfortably?

Looking for solutions

In getting your children to the point of independent behaviour, you will need to strike some sort of balance between suggesting things to them and actually organizing them, as is appropriate. Exactly what you say or do will depend on the situation and the children – or adults – involved.

With young children, the initiative essentially lies with you, and you will need to watch and listen to them in order to build up your own picture of what is going on with them. With older children, however, you can ask them for their insight into the situation, and you should be able simply to prompt them in the right direction.

The learning ladder

With young children you will need to guide their behaviour, teaching them by working up from the first step of the learning ladder. Start by noticing what is happening and coming up with a solution. And then, when they are ready, you can engage them in the process themselves. In summary:

Step One: Observe/watch what is happening. What they need and feel. Arrange a solution you think will meet their needs.

Step Two: When they are old enough, ask them to explain their feelings and needs and help them find a solution.

Step Three: As they get used to this, simply support them in solving the problem themselves.

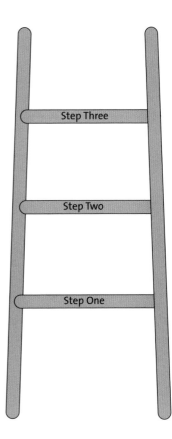

Getting support for ourselves

Most of us have times when parenting presents problems and we need someone sympathetic and supportive to listen to us. Like our children, we need to offload and explore our feelings, share our worries, and reflect on options. Usually friends and family can give us this support, though it may be that we find this inadequate and decide to turn to professionals.

One way to get support is to form a parents' group that meets together on a regular basis to talk over issues and challenges. Or you may prefer to find a particular friend to check in with regularly. You might also like to organize listening sessions.

Listening sessions can be good because they help you to look at problems in a supportive type of atmosphere. A good format for your meeting is, first of all, to take turns to talk about the good things that

THE REFLECTION–ACTION CYCLE

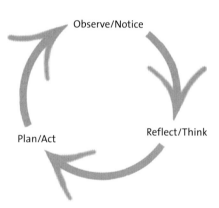

Observe/Notice

Reflect/Think

Plan/Act

How a Reflection–Action cycle works:
Sit in a circle so that you feel comfortable together.
Take turns to share within an agreed time frame.
Without interruptions work through each stage
(see Practical Suggestions opposite):

◊ **Observation:** share what is happening and say how you are feeling – both the good things and the difficult things.

◊ **Reflection:** suggest possible next steps, solutions and plans.

◊ **Action:** decide on the next step and ask for advice or comments.

◊ **Observation:** next time, share what happened, and so on.

have happened and then to take turns to talk about the difficulties. Sharing what we are happy about can lift our spirits, and also it can give us more confidence to share problems. The idea of these groups is to help each person find their own answers to problems, not to hand out unwanted advice, so the focus is on off-loading concerns to a listening audience. If someone would like advice they can ask for suggestions – although the group will need to work out how and when to do this.

A more sophisticated version of a simple listening format is the "Reflection–Action Cycle". This can be a great tool for solving problems or making plans. You start by saying how things are, you reflect on them, and then you decide what to do about them. It is crucial that each person is happy with the plans they make.

> A good format for your meeting is, first of all, to take turns to talk about the good things that have happened and then to take turns to talk about the difficulties.

PRACTICAL SUGGESTIONS

◊ Have ground rules, such as no interrupting, no criticisms, no put-downs. It is important to respect and understand one another.

◊ Have some food and fun. Aim to be positive. Humour and a sense of perspective go a long way to ease tensions, unless there are very big problems under discussion.

◊ Take turns for each person to be heard. One way to do this is for everyone to have a fixed time, such as 15 minutes, to share good and difficult things since the last meeting was held and also to reflect on possible next steps, plans, and solutions.

◊ Be clear how and when you will give each other suggestions. It may well be that as each person talks, they find their own next steps and need no further suggestions. At the end of their 15 minutes they might like to ask for feedback (if you do this you will have to allow time for it).

◊ If someone has a big problem, it may make sense to devote the whole of one meeting to this one issue. It is important to know what you can help with and what you can't.

◊ Use the ideas in this chapter to help you communicate.

Caring and sharing at home helps us develop respect for ourselves, for others, and for our world.

4 Caring and sharing

> ... what we learn as children is the foundation for later life. It is a small but important seed in the building of a more peaceable world.

Building relationships

We learn by doing. Peaceable living involves relating well to one another and doing things together. It means building healthy relationships, celebrating and creating, supporting and sharing, collaborating and caring. Through these experiences we can learn to empathize with others, to understand one another, to find satisfaction and joy in being together.

This section looks at how we can enjoy creating a caring and sharing family. So many pressures in today's world encourage us to be self-centred, to get on with our own lives, to work hard, earn money, focus on what we think is best for us, buy the cheapest we can find, compete for what we want. This can be good for our ambition and our independence, but unless it is tempered with support and caring it can become a selfish and solitary journey.

Caring and sharing within the family may mean laying aside some of these ambitions in order to give more of our attention to being together. Our time and energy are precious. And we may have to make choices so that we can give more to our family and less to other activities. However, this does not mean devoting ourselves entirely to others and becoming compliant "doormats". As we have seen earlier, our own needs matter, too. We need a balance. Space to do what we want is as important as helping others. Time to be quiet is as important as time to be busy. Celebrating and relaxing is as important as getting the routine chores done. A vibrant family life is demanding, but it is also rewarding.

Respect for ourselves, each other, and the planet

Caring and sharing at home helps us develop respect for ourselves, for others, and for our world. It gives us self-respect, connection, and meaning so that we have the confidence to work well with others. We learn to appreciate and encourage one another's unique qualities and talents. What we create in the family ripples outward, because what we learn as children is the foundation for later life. It is a small but important seed in the building of a more peaceable world.

Time together

To create a peaceable family it is important to have times when everyone can come together to share, to talk, to enjoy one another's company. The ordinary activities make up the fabric of everyday life. If we do not share them, we lose touch with one another. We stop living together.

A simple daily rhythm of a few shared activities is all it takes; we do not have to live in each other's pockets. Yet in the hustle and bustle of modern life, this can so easily be forgotten. Can you find three times in an average day when you can be together, preferably having fun?

SHARING TIMES
◊ Breakfast
◊ Snacks
◊ Lunch
◊ Tea
◊ Story time
◊ Play time
◊ After school
◊ Bedtime

SHARED MEALS

Shared meals are a great way to meet and chat. It's a habit that is worth re-creating if you have lost it. Eating together can be a delight, a time to talk, to affirm one another, to slow down, perhaps.

Making shared meals a regular habit

◊ Choose a time that fits everyone's needs, as far as you can. If you all have busy schedules, try just three or four shared meals a week – or whatever makes sense.

◊ Make sure everyone is comfortable – that chairs are a good height, for example.

◊ Start with food everyone likes. Introduce new foods gradually.

◊ If everyone likes different things, take turns to choose.

◊ Involve everybody in the preparation, if you can, so that they take pleasure in producing the food or laying the table.

◊ Go for food that is healthy, releasing energy gradually so you don't need to snack too often.

◊ Present the food as attractively as possible.

◊ Encourage everyone to talk during the meal so that it feels good to be together.

◊ When you have a problem, relax and think laterally!

Bedtime

Regular bedtimes help us to unwind. Like mealtimes, you may need to be flexible while still keeping to a normal pattern most of the time. Most of us know how good it is to go to sleep feeling warm, relaxed, and comfortable about ourselves. When your child is ready for bed, you can help create this kind of atmosphere.

Tips for a good bedtime routine
◊ Talk over the good things of the day.
◊ Tell or read a story together.
◊ Play quiet music or sing songs.
◊ Be reassuring and comforting.
◊ Have a cuddle and say goodnight.

If a child is restless, you may find that prayer – or your version of prayer – can help settle her because it is way to give our thanks and to express our hopes. You can create your own non-religious prayer, for example, by remembering the good things of the day that has just gone and by thinking about the positive opportunities of the day to come. It will also help to remind her that she is loved and that you are near by. If your child has questions or worries, it is important to address them, but preferably earlier in the day.

AT STORY TIME
Ask yourself:

◊ Who are the heroes and heroines?
◊ What do they do?
◊ How do they solve problems?
◊ What does the outcome of the story convey?
◊ What values and lessons does the story teach?
◊ And are these what you want for your children?

Story time

Reading aloud or telling stories is a great way to share ideas, develop empathy, and broaden horizons. This is a chance to travel together in our imaginations, to shape ideas and ideals. Remember, stories have messages. Those with violent heroes and plots encourage us to assume that violence is inevitable. Stories that engage our empathy and generosity show us another way.

Quiet time

A quiet time can be a great way to restore peace and calm in a crisis. It's also good to make a habit of being quiet together. When we are truly quiet and still, we can discover a sense of deep, calm space inside of ourselves that helps us to find an inner confidence.

If you can show a child what it is like to be quiet and still, you are giving her a wonderful gift. It can help her to feel rooted in herself and clear about who she is and what matters to her, while at the same time she can be open and understanding of others.

The practice of stillness can help us all to cope with the ordinary challenges of life, such as awkward meetings or fraught phone calls. The sense of inner peace that stillness brings can give us the personal power to deal with these difficult situations. In the middle of an argument, it can help dissipate anger and aggression in others as well as ourselves. Perhaps we can stop ourselves getting sucked into the anger and panic and, instead, see how we can help constructively.

> The practice of stillness can help us all to cope with the ordinary challenges of life.

QUIET FAMILY TIMES

◊ Sit quietly together in a circle and ask everyone simply to listen and watch. If you are in the garden, you might hear the sounds of traffic and other people, or of birds. You might see plants or washing blowing in the wind. After a few minutes, you can tell each other what you have noticed.

◊ Look out for stretching exercises for children that help them to be quietly aware of their own bodies. Lie down to relaxing music. Or go a further step and introduce your family to yoga.

◊ Go for walks and notice the tallest, strongest trees. Then come home and practise being a tree, rooted in the ground, swaying gently in the breeze. Next time you are caught up in a panic, try to remember what it is like to be as rooted and as flexible as a tree.

◊ Music affects our mood. Some music is conducive to concentration, some to relaxation, and some to movement. If you or your children play background music, see if you can encourage what seems appropriate for the activity and time of day.

◊ Bring quiet times into everyday life. Perhaps you can have a silent moment before meals or before you start an activity, such as music practice or homework.

> When we follow our instincts and do the things that we love, we feel good about ourselves, we learn fast, and we explore eagerly.

Working together

In a peaceable family, it is important to have activities that people cooperate on. A joint activity teaches us so much about each other and how we can share our time and energy. However, it can be tough. Sometimes we get into arguments that make huge demands on our communication skills; sometimes we just run out of patience and wish we were doing the job on our own. There have been many times when I felt like doing the activity on my own. But the skills of cooperation are particularly useful and the rewards are definitely worth working for. When we do something well together we all feel appreciated and life is great.

Making or doing things together is important because:

◊ It is a good way to learn from one another – adults can learn from children, as well as the other way around.

◊ It helps us communicate as we work; we can discuss alternatives and come up with what seems best.

◊ We get to know each other in different ways by contributing our various ideas and skills.

◊ It is good practice for later life because we learn to work with others in a team and understand different perspectives.

Family projects

One way to reduce the frustrations and irritations of working together is to find a project that everyone can enjoy doing. Interest and enjoyment are themselves an incentive. When we follow our instincts and do the things that we love, we feel good about ourselves, we learn fast, and we explore eagerly. At the same time, everyone can be learning together, sharing skills and experience, taking turns, and being a team.

If you are not sure what projects to do with your children, why not watch them and reflect on what they seem to like doing best?

Some project ideas

◊ Making scrapbooks or posters can be great fun because everyone can collect what they like and then think of their own ways to display what they've done. Some families mix photographs, drawings, tickets, maps, diary entries, and messages that reflect everyone's experiences and interests. I still have my holiday scrapbooks from my early travels in Europe.

◊ Looking after pets or plants teaches children about caring. You can look after them together or give each child their own task, according to their age and ability.

◊ Sharing an interest in a particular type of music or sport can involve everyone in some way, perhaps practising together, learning about performers or players, going to events, and getting to know people with similar interests. Of course this is ambitious and will not work for everyone.

FAMILY PROJECT WEBCHART

DRAWING
◊ Pictures to stick on the kitchen wall
◊ Scrapbooks
◊ Making birthday cards
◊ Writing
◊ Taking photographs

COLLECTING
◊ Model cars or toys
◊ Card sets
◊ Coins
◊ Stickers

WHAT DO THEY LIKE DOING?

GARDENING
◊ Making a mini garden
◊ Planting seeds
◊ Caring for pot plants
◊ Topping up the compost

BALL GAMES
◊ Playing ball games regularly
◊ Joining the junior basket ball, tennis, or soccer club

CELEBRATING
◊ Making decorations
◊ Baking cakes
◊ Singing
◊ Dancing

When things get stuck

Sometimes, even with the best planning in the world, things get stuck, someone is bored or frustrated. Here are some tips to help you when you encounter a sticky patch.

Notice if the task is appropriate for the child to cope with. Is it a pleasure or a chore, a bit of a challenge, or just too much?

Encourage what went well. "This card is really cheerful and bright." If it wasn't quite right, explain how you would like it to look. "That is a great start! I think this piece of card needs to be a little smaller."

Look for improvements together. "That took a long time, didn't it? How do you think we can do it quicker next time?"

Enjoy doing it with them and give the job your attention. Draw your own holiday picture for the noticeboard and leave your child to do her own. This can be a wonderful way to remember your holiday together.

If you are really stuck, abandon the first task and try doing something different instead. Remember – there is no such thing as failure. Only feedback and learning.

AFFIRMING AND ENCOURAGING

This card is really cheerful and bright.

Do you like my card?
What can I do to make it better?

This is a great start!

I think this piece of card needs to be a little smaller.

Shall we put this on the board so we can all enjoy it?

The pros and cons of competition

Competition generates conflict. This may not be a bad thing, as it depends on the context, the purpose, and the effect of it. There is a world of difference between the type of competition that divides and drives people to outdo each other and that which unites and encourages people to do their best.

The problem with competition is that it creates winners and losers. This will always happen, because that is what competition is all about. Some people rise to the challenge. Those who are constantly the loser become de-energized and lethargic or resentful and bitter. This does not help anyone to become comfortable, caring, or capable. So competition, like punishment and rewards, needs to be used with great care.

SUCCESSFUL COMPETITION

That was fun!   We're getting good at this.

We did really well!   Let's do it again!

UNSUCCESSFUL COMPETITION

That was great!

I'm bored with this ... I'm going.

That was stupid ... I'm off!

That's not fair!

Competition working well

To help our children handle competition well, they need to experience it. Otherwise it will be a great shock when they meet it in the outside world. They do need to be able to get in there and join in. They also need to be able to say when it is not working for them. Many people think that competition is good because it encourages us to do our best. But it is better still when we do something well because we have taken care and pleasure in it. Real reward comes from feeling good inside ourselves because this was something we really enjoyed and felt we did our best with.

Watch and listen to see how your children respond to competition

You can ask yourself: are they enjoying it; is any-one suffering; what is good or bad about it? It's probably fine when it fosters team-building, when it encourages us to do our best, and when everyone is enjoying themselves.

If someone is unhappy about the competition, go back and have a look at the previous chapter to see how you might help her communicate her feelings and needs.

Of course, competition can always be modified. We can encourage our children to aim for their own standards or targets, to win certificates for themselves, to beat their previous best, and to rise to a challenge – such as a testing walk or a personal best. We can help them to compete at a level where they are comfortable, so that everybody wins sometimes.

It is also good to encourage teamwork, so that children learn to share the efforts and rewards of doing something with others. Being in a team helps participants learn to give and take, to appreciate the skills of others, and to share responsibility. Ultimately a team depends on everyone being able to solve problems together; it's a great way to practise peace-making.

Alternatives to competition

Competition may not always be appropriate or healthy. If we constantly expect our child to do well, what message are we giving her? Are we putting too much pressure on her? Is she fearful of failure? Or are we teaching her that success is just in winning? Is this the cause of sibling rivalry?

When there is a lot of rivalry between children, quietly watch them and see what you can do to reduce its occurrence. As we have already seen, children who are always trying to outdo each other need to be affirmed for themselves as they are. You can encourage activities that are rewarding in themselves, such as projects and hobbies. Play, creative arts, and celebration are also important, because they can be open-ended and dynamic, creative, and energizing.

With our twins, we found it helped enormously to encourage them in their own particular interests. Our son enjoyed ball games and constructing things. Our daughter was happy with drawing, games, and stories. Neither seemed particularly good at what the other did well and both resented this a little. However, we tried hard to avoid comparison and encouraged what they loved. Their resentment melted as they got on with what they enjoyed doing best.

> ...children who are always trying to outdo each other need to be affirmed for themselves as they are. You can encourage activities that are rewarding in themselves...

Sharing our joy

Sharing our joy is an essential part of peace-making. It helps us to develop full lives; it also helps us to appreciate one another and to love being together.

Some of us feel that life is all about duty or hard work and that there is something "wrong" with doing what we really enjoy. Life may be better in the future, but only if we work hard for it in the present. However, in reality life is for living now and we need to enjoy it now if we possibly can.

In fact, what we enjoy doing is really important, because it is often a clue to our gifts and skills. A child who loves puzzles and making models is learning skills that may lead toward crafts, engineering, or architecture, whereas a child who loves collecting leaves and growing plants may develop a passion for gardening or the environment. Sometimes we look endlessly outside ourselves for enjoyment, through shopping, drinking, watching TV, and many other activities. But unless we find joy inside ourselves or in our own creativity, we are unlikely ever to be truly happy and at ease with ourselves. The more pleasure a child has in life, the more confidently she will reach out to new interests and activities as she grows up.

Sharing our joy is an essential part of peace-making. It helps us to develop full lives; it also helps us to appreciate one another and to love being together.

Playing together

Play is not simply sitting quietly with a jigsaw or stacking up bricks. Unlike watching TV, which is essentially a passive activity, play is active, untidy, informal, and it engages us fully. Play is about getting in there and becoming involved. Play time is essential for children to experiment with relationships, play back what they are learning, and push out some of their boundaries. It is an opportunity to share, to take turns, to cooperate, to learn empathy, and to stretch their imaginations, to argue and negotiate, to see other points of view. Play is children's work, but it is important for adults, too.

Play doesn't need loads of toys. In fact, too many toys are confusing because it is more difficult for a child to choose and focus or to value and respect what she has. Play needs appropriate toys that open the imagination and help develop skills.

Children don't have to share all the time. Most children need some things that are specially their own, that they particularly love and treasure and learn to look after. We need to teach them to respect this and appreciate what is special for others. However, it is also important that they learn about generosity, so that they enjoy sharing and giving and receiving.

Play that lights the imagination is crucial because it helps children to learn about relating to one another. Some children are more deeply drawn to imaginative play than others. As a child I loved going on imaginary adventures with my sister and writing stories with drawings to go with them. Other children like to act out everyday things, such as shopping, or they pretend to be celebrities. They can pretend to be other people, to explore alternative scenarios, to test reactions in a safe, experimental setting. They can create together with no fixed goal or purpose.

Children's play is influenced by TV and books, as well as by everyday life. As a parent, you can influence children by making suggestions about what to do next or by choosing the things they play with.

> Play time is essential for children to experiment with relationships, play back what they are learning, and push out some of their boundaries.

TIPS FOR IMAGINATIVE PLAY

◊ Collect dressing-up props from charity clothes shops – or make them yourself from odd bits and pieces.

◊ Think laterally about the things you already have in your cupboards. Bought toys often provide less scope for the imagination because they are tailor-made – pots and pans can be great drums or containers, while cardboard boxes can make a wonderful den, car, or train.

◊ Tell your children stories that kindle their imagination with heroes and heroines who encourage positive, peaceable messages.

◊ Join in and develop your role-play skills. Encourage them to ask, "What if?" questions so that they think creatively about alternatives.

> When we celebrate important occasions, we can look for the core meaning that unites us and affirms our common humanity.

Celebrating together

Most celebrations are an opportunity to come together to connect with others, to affirm ourselves, and to express our thanks. Occasions such as birthdays, christenings, baptisms, barmitzvahs, and confirmations affirm us as individuals. In most traditions, even a funeral is in one sense an affirmation because it is, in part at least, a thanksgiving for a person's life. These are all rites of passage, in which we acknowledge that life moves on and we are growing up. Annual festivals of the religious calendar also affirm us because they celebrate common values, traditions, and beliefs.

The core meaning

The rituals of celebrations can divide people, perhaps because they are specific to a particular faith and also perhaps because they are based on the belief that there is only one "right" way to "God". Peaceable living seeks to build bridges by acknowledging that behind the rituals lie the seeds of compassion and forgiveness.

When we celebrate important occasions, we can look for the core meaning that unites us and affirms our common humanity. For example, peeling away the hype around Christmas enables remembering the potential of love and healing that Jesus taught. Holy days such as the Sabbath and Sundays traditionally were days of coming together to worship and celebrate community. We may not wish to take part in the prayers, but we might find it helpful to put aside time to be together, to be quiet, perhaps, to catch up with one another's news, or do something special together.

Creating our own celebration

It's good to create celebrations in our own way, whenever we wish, however we wish. Perhaps we want to welcome a newcomer, to give thanks, or to send our best wishes. The variety of special greetings cards in the stores gives you a flavour of the possibilities.

Children love to celebrate, to decorate the table or the room, to make cards and presents, to cook special food. The ritual can be simple. Perhaps there can be a few candles or flowers in the room. Or someone can tell a story or sing. Candles in the darkness are a symbol of hope and new life, which we can all relate to. At the beginning of February, I used to light candles to cheer us in the coldest time of the London year. In the Christian calendar, this is Epiphany, the time when Jesus was welcomed at the temple, but on a universal level it is a time when we can all celebrate new beginnings. In our family we also celebrated Valentine's Day on February 14. Today, it seems to be yet another occasion when the shops are full of cards and flowers, but behind the growing commercialization of this simple event there is again a universal message. Both our children enjoyed expressing their love by making cards for everyone in the family.

Planning a celebration

◊ Birthdays are significant for each of us, but birthday parties can be a real headache.
Can you step back for a moment and ask yourself what is realistically practical?
You don't have to be a martyr. Perhaps you can invite parents as well as children so you don't have to look after a dozen excited four-year-olds on your own.

◊ Many festivals are another occasion to spend lots of money.
Are there cheap or free ways of celebrating?
Can you see behind the festive front to the real meaning?
In the West, Christmas invades the whole community, regardless of religious sensitivities, and we find ourselves sucked into it whether we like it or not. Perhaps we can create our own celebration in which we give simple gifts to our friends and family.
Some families place a spending limit on all presents.

◊ Sad times in a family are also important. Hiding our grief will not make it go away. Can you bring a personal touch to a funeral that affirms the life that is gone and the distress of those bereaved?
Perhaps after the formal service you can make your own ceremony with a quiet remembering or with an activity that the deceased person would have enjoyed.

◊ Creating your own celebration is empowering and fun.
What do you value in your life that you would like to affirm?
If shared meals are difficult to arrange during the week, perhaps you can have a weekly meal together to celebrate the family as a whole. Many people do this for Sunday lunch or on Friday night.

> When we take responsibility we are in charge of our lives, we are accomplishing something, and we may be helping someone.

Sharing responsibilities

Taking responsibility can be fun, affirming, and satisfying. When we take responsibility we are in charge of our lives, we are accomplishing something, and we may be helping someone. It is an essential part of the peaceable family because responsibility gradually becomes a joint activity.

As most of us know only too well, it's often not as simple as that. Handing over responsibility to others is often accompanied by complaints and arguments. And we ask ourselves, why do we bother? Well, it is important because that is how we become independent, autonomous people. So we need to find a way to encourage our children to share responsibility, however time-consuming and frustrating.

This is important because, in later life, we want our children to derive pleasure and satisfaction from taking responsibility. We would rather they did not see responsibility as a drudge or a worry. So start now, as soon as you can, to give them a sense of purpose and accomplishment.

The learning ladder revisited
The way to start is to share responsibility

Some children learn by copying and are helpful by nature. Others need to be taught and encouraged.

It helps to learn by doing things together so that they understand what you want.

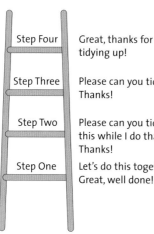

Step Four — Great, thanks for tidying up!

Step Three — Please can you tidy up? Thanks!

Step Two — Please can you tidy this while I do that? Thanks!

Step One — Let's do this together. Great, well done!

Step One: Start by choosing a task that you can do together, such as putting away toys. Have fun doing this and give praise.

Step Two: As this becomes a habit, ask them to do one bit while you do another, so you are alongside to encourage them.

Step Three: Next, ask them to pack everything away, but hang around to affirm and encourage.

Step Four: Now they can take responsibility.

Mind the gap

Of course, nothing in real life is as simple as that. There is usually a gap between what we would like our children to do and what they actually do (and perhaps this applies to our partner, too).

First of all look to see if your child thinks the tasks are useful, doable, and satisfying.
◊ Does she think they are useful?
◊ Does she see the point of doing them?
◊ Has she got the skills and time to do them?
◊ Is there an element of enjoyment and satisfaction in the tasks?

There may be other questions you wish to ask.

If the answer to any of your questions is "No", go back to the drawing board and think how you can rearrange the tasks you have given her, so you can narrow the gap as much as possible. In my experience the greatest pleasure is in doing things together. Cooking meals with one child at a time was great because we could work out menus we both liked.

A good way to discuss issues of responsibility is to have regular family discussions, where you talk about the good things as well as the difficult things, perhaps over a meal (see p. 75).

What we learn
at home is the
foundation for
living beyond it –
a resource for life.

5 Being capable

> When we teach a child the skills of peaceable living within the family, we are giving him a resource he will be able to turn to any time, anywhere.

Resources for life

So far we have looked at how we can help our children to be comfortable with themselves, caring of others and good at communicating their needs and feelings. What we learn at home is the foundation for living beyond it – a resource for life.

When we teach a child the skills of peaceable living within the family, we are giving him a resource he will be able to turn to any time, anywhere. However, these are not abilities we learn in a few months, or even years. It is a continuing process that involves developing attitudes, habits and skills that all help us to relate well to one another and make things happen. Helping our children to develop this capability is fun and rewarding.

Peaceable living is a way of life. It helps us to:
◊ Respect ourselves.
◊ Relate to others.
◊ Resolve problems.
And it does all this in ways that acknowledge our different ideas, experiences, and needs.

One of the challenges is knowing when to encourage a child to take more responsibility and how much support to give, if any. Sometimes we can set our expectations too high for a child's present capability and, as a consequence, he may feel pressurized or inadequate. Alternatively, we may discourage him so that he does not develop the resources to manage well on his own. We need to find a balance between taking charge ourselves and giving him a complete free rein. Different situations require a different balance and different skills.

Ideas and tools in this section can help us all – adults as well as children – to live peaceably, not only in the family, but also in the different situations we find ourselves in.

Power – handle with care

Being capable is partly an issue of power and partly of responsibility. If we look at different groups or organizations we can see there are different types of power. In a school, for example, a teacher may discipline the class firmly with put-downs, threats, and punishments. Alternatively the teacher may create a sense of collective responsibility through explanation and example. The first type of teacher uses a culture of fear to maintain discipline; he has power over the children. The second type of teacher creates a culture of responsibility and cooperation. In his class, power is shared. The children are respected and they can concentrate on learning skills, making good choices, and relating well to others. When they learn these skills, they develop the power to do things themselves and the power together to help create a good atmosphere in the class.

Developing "power to" and "power together" is an important key to peaceable living. Taking "power over" someone may be necessary in a crisis – when people are being hurt, for example. But on the whole, it is a recipe for distress and conflict.

"POWER OVER"

Do as I say!
This is good for you.

No! It's not fair!

Oh dear!

The bitch!

"POWER TO" AND "POWER TOGETHER"

This is fun!

Shall I do this?

Let's do this together.

Can I help?

> When you set out to show and share your skills with a child you will be giving him the power to do something for himself.

"Power over" is not peaceable

It is all too easy to take control of difficult situations, thinking we know best or just because it seems simpler. Making this a habit, however, is likely to cause problems. We may feel great to be in charge, but we may also feel worn out or that we are the family martyr or slave. In the meantime, our children may find it more difficult to take responsibility for themselves, even feeling resentful, frustrated, or helpless. And they may not get much chance to learn about independence.

To control them we might threaten, punish, criticize, or belittle them. This may also involve violence. But as a habit, it is likely to build an atmosphere of distress, fear, or defiance. This is a form of bullying.

In some situations, children develop the skills of taking power over others. When children are rude, defiant, or violent they are trying to take control. Taken to extremes, children like this may become a danger to themselves and their community. Studies of children who have killed or injured others reveal that they were not given limits to their own power, so had little understanding of the consequences of their actions.

"Power to" and "power together" are peaceable

It is essential to teach our children a different kind of power. When we help them to take responsibility, to make good decisions, and to express themselves well we are giving them the power to organize and shape their lives. When we show them how to do this with others, we are helping them to discover "power together". And when they have a sense of their own worth and are in touch with their own feelings, they discover "power within". They know what it means to respect others and themselves.

Peaceable parenting means helping children to acquire the skills they need to acquire these kinds of power. Can you think of times when your child was actively involved in this way? Perhaps he was absorbed in an activity or was playing creatively with others. When I am working well with others, I feel at ease and also excited, with a sense of uplift and pleasure. I just know that the outcome will be good! What about you? What does "power together" feel like for you?

REMEMBER

◊ When someone takes control as a habit they have "power over" others.

◊ When people learn skills, they acquire the "power to" do something.

◊ When they join together to make decisions and do things, they have "power together".

Show and share your skills

When you set out to show and share your skills with a child you will be giving him the "power to" do something for himself. This may take time, but it will almost always be worth it. For example, if you show a child how to mix paints and to clean the brushes and the paint pots you are giving him the skills to look after them himself. He will learn with confidence. But if you always do it for him or just leave them dirty, you are preventing him from learning something useful.

Showing and sharing may require patience, but we can find a lot of joy in simply slowing down and giving our attention to a child who is learning. If we watch, we can probably see how he learns best. Does he watch and copy you? Does he like to get into it quickly and try for himself? Does he like something that is easy and then does he get more adventurous?

We each have our preferred ways of learning and working. For example, when I try to assemble something, my first instinct is to get hold of all the pieces and see how they might fit together. Only then do I read the instructions. Young children tend to be mainly visual and kinesthetic in their approach, so they learn by watching and doing. Notice as they get older whether they are happy to read instructions or whether they prefer to be shown.

The learning ladder revisited

Sometimes he will learn quickly and at other times you will have to teach one step at a time, as in this example:

Step One: Show your child how to mix paints and clean the brushes. Do this at a pace he can understand.
Step Two: When he has a go, be willing to be patient. Do it together – share the activity – if that seems sensible.
Step Three: Encourage him to have a go on his own, but be there as a support for him.

Step Three — Let him do it and keep an eye on how he does it.

Step Two — Do it together.

Step One — Show him how to do it.

> The more we are able to manage our choices, the more confident and capable we feel.

Active choices

One of the most useful peacemaking skills is the ability to see what choices we have. Many arguments develop because we each think *we* have the answer. Either we think we know best or we have not stopped to think things out as thoroughly as we could.

In fact, we are always making choices, whether we notice it or not: when to get up in the morning; what to eat; where to cross the road; what to say to our friends. Many of us have mixed feelings about choice. If you think about this for a moment, can you recall choices you have made and choices you have missed? Sometimes we agonize over what to do and whether we did the right thing yesterday. At other times we feel helpless because we think we have no choice. Sometimes we just get on with life without realizing how much we can choose and, therefore, how much control and influence we can have over our lives. In between, there is a happy medium where we recognize our choices and know how much time and energy to give them. The more we are able to manage our choices, the more confident and capable we feel.

No one right way

Let's look at this more closely. Many arguments and conflicts develop because we think there is only one right view or one right way to do something. This perspective is a major obstacle to seeing what our choices are. It is a tunnel-vision view of life that blinkers us and prevents us understanding others.

Of course, where there is some sort of a technical or legal problem to be solved, there may well be only one correct solution – but in most areas of life, there may be several good ways to do something and no absolutely perfect way.

The idea that there must always be a right way or a right view can be very disempowering. Perhaps somebody makes a proposal that we are not entirely happy with. We think they know better than us, so we choose to accept their idea on the grounds that they must be right and we must be wrong. Or, alternatively, we think their idea is rubbish and jump in with our own proposal, which we think is far better. Both of these responses are underpinned by the supposition that there is only one right way to proceed.

Once we let go of this fiction, we can change direction and come up with lots of good ways, which can be pooled to make a new and better solution that no one had thought of.

WHICH WAY?

When we think there is only one right way, we find it difficult to consider alternatives.

When we see several possibilities, we may find a solution everyone likes.

What are the possibilities?

Can we combine them?

Can we find a "best fit"?

Choosing is good for us

Generating choices is an essential part of peacemaking. In most situations we have some power of choice. Even when we believe that we have absolutely none at all, we may surprise ourselves once we start to look more carefully. It can help us clear the air, feel better, and make good things happen.

One way to help a child to generate choices is to ask "What if . . . ?" For example, suppose he would like to make a birthday card using white card and coloured tissue paper. There is card in the drawer, but no tissue paper anywhere in the house. If you say "Let's see what other ideas we can come up with", you are immediately opening up choices. You can start the ball rolling by saying "What if . . . ?", and then encourage him to come up with his own ideas. The more he can generate alternatives, the more he is likely to come up with his own solutions. However, in this particular example it might be wise to see what materials you do have available before he starts making any alternative suggestions.

REMEMBER

Writing ideas down or drawing them, such as in the webchart below, can be great fun as well as being useful in more complex situations – such as where to go on holiday or how to rearrange a room.

CHOICES WEBCHART

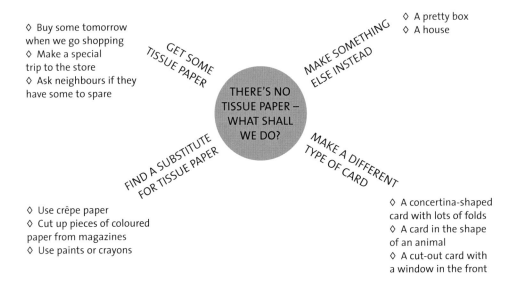

◊ Buy some tomorrow when we go shopping
◊ Make a special trip to the store
◊ Ask neighbours if they have some to spare

GET SOME TISSUE PAPER

MAKE SOMETHING ELSE INSTEAD

◊ A pretty box
◊ A house

THERE'S NO TISSUE PAPER – WHAT SHALL WE DO?

FIND A SUBSTITUTE FOR TISSUE PAPER

MAKE A DIFFERENT TYPE OF CARD

◊ Use crêpe paper
◊ Cut up pieces of coloured paper from magazines
◊ Use paints or crayons

◊ A concertina-shaped card with lots of folds
◊ A card in the shape of an animal
◊ A cut-out card with a window in the front

When to offer choices

There are, of course, times when it is not appropriate to encourage lots of choices. It may be that the best thing you can do is to take charge and say firmly what is going to happen next. Arguments and quarrels may develop because there is too much choice and we can't make up our minds or we just cannot agree. As with any skill, teaching a child to choose well involves being aware of his ability and offering appropriate choices, so that he learns at his own pace.

Three-year-olds who are asked to choose from the whole menu in a café are likely to be demanding or anxious because there are too many options and too much is expected of them. A parent's intention may be to encourage them to make choices, but when the burden is too great they will be overwhelmed and unable to decide for themselves.

However, when there seems to be no choice we can also be frustrated and angry. In reality there are almost always some choices or some possibility of choice. The minute we look more carefully, the situation becomes more hopeful. Making an active choice is a skill like any other. It means thinking laterally and creatively, considering your own needs and those of others – turning things on their head, perhaps. We need to demonstrate and teach it, as appropriate.

> Making an active choice is a skill like any other. It means thinking laterally and creatively, considering your own needs and those of others . . .

The learning ladder revisited
How to offer choices

In the example of choosing from the menu at a café, it is probably best to scan the menu first yourself and then offer children two or three choices, or take the next step, which is to look at it together. Alternatively, you could go to a café that offers an abbreviated children's menu. Teach the method one step at a time.

Step Three

Step Two

Step One

Step One: Offer two or three realistic options.
Step Two: Offer more choices when they are ready – and talk about them.
Step Three: Encourage them to come up with their own choices and talk about them.

Turnaround thinking

We have already seen how we respond to conflicts in different ways (see p. 15). We can summarize these as:

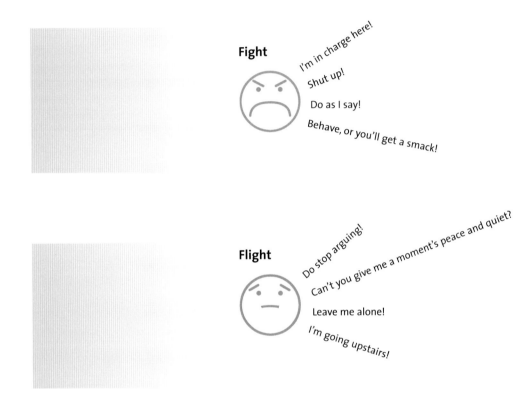

Fight

I'm in charge here!

Shut up!

Do as I say!

Behave, or you'll get a smack!

Flight

Do stop arguing!

Can't you give me a moment's peace and quiet?

Leave me alone!

I'm going upstairs!

Turnaround

This behaviour won't do.

What are we going to do about this?

Calm down.

Please tell me what's going on.

I understand how you're feeling.

THE NEGATIVE SPIRAL

When we respond to a conflict by going into "fight mode" we are creating a negative cycle. We feed the conflict with our energy and go into a spiral in which tensions build up until, finally, something snaps or explodes. Someone loses their temper or something gets broken.

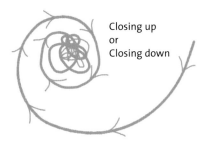

Closing up
or
Closing down

THE POSITIVE SPIRAL

"Turnaround thinking" means that we calm down and stop putting our energy into this negative spiral. We turn our energy around into a positive spiral and ask ourselves how we can do this differently. We turn around our thinking and look at the opposite view. We open ourselves to other possibilities and generate alternatives. The tension disperses.

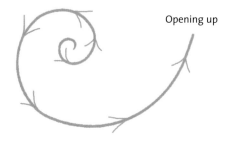

Opening up

Turnaround solutions

In most situations we do have a choice – you can see a problem either as a crisis or as an opportunity. Either we can get more and more angry or we can stop and listen and look for alternative responses. Turnaround thinking is an opportunity to solve problems in a constructive fashion in order to understand one another better and perhaps to care for each other more.

TURNAROUND THINKING

◊ Discourages the *either/or* type of thinking, which only keeps the argument going.
◊ Encourages the *both/and* type of thinking, which opens up alternatives. It can free us up, allowing us to start to be creative and positive.
Try it and see!

To turn the energy around we need to:
◊ STOP arguing.
◊ UNDERSTAND what is going on.
◊ LOOK for choices and solutions.

QUICK TURNAROUND EXAMPLE
Suppose two children are playing together
and then they start to fight.

STOP!
Arguing

This may not be easy to begin with. You will need to engage with each of them, make eye contact, and speak to each separately. Once they know you will help them solve the problem, they will be more willing to listen to you.

◊ Find a way to stop them.
◊ Make eye contact.
◊ Put your hands on their shoulders.

UNDERSTAND!
Watch, listen, and notice

◊ Are they tired?
◊ Bored?
◊ Hungry?
◊ Is one child dominating?
◊ Is one child bullying?

LOOK!
For solutions based on needs

Do they need:

◊ To stop playing
Does either of them need a rest or food? Or a quiet time?

◊ To share
Can you find another toy or game that is easier for them to share?

◊ To play separately
Can you find things they can do on their own?

◊ To be with you
Are they asking for time with you?

Not-so-quick turnaround

You can use turnaround thinking for big problems as well as small ones. "Turnaround" means looking for choices from a new perspective, or turning our current thinking on its head. Can we combine any of the ideas or adapt one of them? Do we have a new idea that will suit everyone? If there is still no agreement, can we take turns to choose in future? If not, perhaps the original issue is not so important after all – for example, perhaps you don't all want to go out together after all! Go back to *Active choices* (see pp. 96–7) or forward to *Consensus decision-making* (see pp. 104–7) for more ideas about finding solutions.

> Turnaround means looking for choices from a new perspective, or turning our current thinking on its head.

REMEMBER

◊ The basis of turnaround is to turn the energy around.
◊ Stop thinking that the solution must be either one thing *or* the other.
◊ Start opening up and begin to think that perhaps the solution can be both one *and* the other.

The learning ladder revisited

Use the learning ladder steps to teach children to find their own solutions, when they are ready (see also pp. 69, 88, 95, and 99).

Step One: Give them a solution.
Step Two: Offer solutions.
Step Three: Help them find a solution.

Step Three   Have a think about
the best way to do it.

Step Two   You could do it this
way or that way.

Step One   Do it this way.

Consensus decision-making

Consensus decision-making is a strategy you might find useful for more complex decisions. The underlying assumption is that everyone is willing to sit down and talk because they want to reach a decision everyone will be happy with. This may not be possible, but they are willing to try. You can use this method when there are several ideas and possibly some areas of disagreement.

> In consensus decision-making, everyone is involved and every view is considered. A conscious effort is made to reach a decision that works and that everyone feels is satisfactory.

Good times to use consensus decision-making:
◊ When making vacation plans.
◊ Deciding how to decorate a room.
◊ Choosing a new pet.
◊ Prioritizing time.
◊ Solving household task issues.

In consensus decision-making, everyone is involved and every view is considered. A conscious effort is made to reach a decision that works and that everyone feels is satisfactory. When you make a decision that has everyone's support, there will be a high degree of commitment to the project.

How to reach a decision by consensus

You need to put aside a time and place to do this well. Ask everyone to sit down so that everyone can make eye contact. In this way there is no boss saying: "We will do this!" Nor is there any voting, where only the majority get what they want. However, someone will need to be the facilitator. This person can express a point of view, but cannot impose it.

Three steps of consensus decision-making

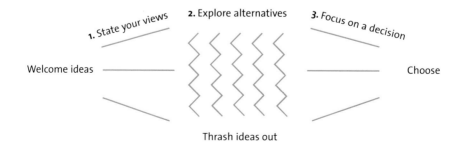

1. State your views 2. Explore alternatives 3. Focus on a decision

Welcome ideas — Choose

Thrash ideas out

There are three steps to this process. How you work through them is up to you. Here are some suggestions:

Step 1 State your views

When everyone is gathered, the facilitator asks each person in turn to say what they think, while everyone else listens attentively without interruption or criticism. It may help to write down what each person says on a large piece of paper so that everybody can see what everyone else is thinking.

If there is a lot of disagreement the facilitator has several options. He can summarize what he has heard so that everyone feels they are understood. Or he may ask each person to share their feelings and needs by making an "I" statement (see p. 62) This can be good because it is easier to empathize with people when they speak from their own point of view and focus on what they feel. If someone has no view, they can pass or speak later. If someone talks a lot, the facilitator can propose a time limit. The rules are made by the group to suit the group's needs.

Step 2 Explore alternatives

Once everyone has shared their thoughts, it is a good idea to discuss their preferences and then look at the pros and cons. This way you can understand each other and perhaps be convinced. If the ideas are written down on a sheet of paper, everyone can comment on the list. It's a good idea to clump similar ideas together and then add any new ones as they are introduced.

Useful questions to ask are:
◊ What do you feel about each idea?
◊ Can you tell us why you think this?
◊ What would happen if we did this one or that one?
◊ Apart from your own idea, which do you like most?

If everyone is talking at once, the facilitator can ask each person to speak in turn.

Step 3 Focus on a decision

Once people understand the reasons for a particular suggestion and really engage with the consequences, they are more likely to find a common way forward. When the facilitator thinks that everyone has reached that point of understanding, he can summarize what he has heard and check that he has got it right. It may be that he can spot one idea that he thinks everyone would be happy with, or he may see a pattern and a solution emerging. If so, he can ask then what everyone thinks of it. Alternatively, he can ask everyone to see if they can see a solution now that they have heard all of the views and ideas.

If no solution emerges, it may help to stop for the time being and leave everyone to think it over. You could look at some of the other ideas in this book and see if any of them would help.

WHEN CONSENSUS DECISION-MAKING WORKS WELL

Combining varying wishes

Everyone wants to go somewhere different
Consensus decision-making can lead to creative solutions combining everyone's ideas. Chris, Jo, Frank, and Elaine are planning a vacation and each suggests a different destination – Chris wants a beach holiday, Jo a theme park, Frank likes castles and old villages, while Elaine wants a place to relax. They each explain why they are keen on their idea, so that they all understand each other. Then they think about how to adapt their ideas and where else they could go. This opens up the possibility of a place that suits them all. Perhaps they could go to a coastal village with old buildings of interest and great activity centres to visit near by.

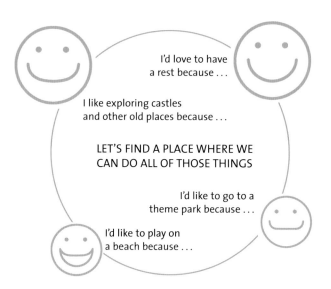

I'd love to have a rest because . . .

I like exploring castles and other old places because . . .

LET'S FIND A PLACE WHERE WE CAN DO ALL OF THOSE THINGS

I'd like to go to a theme park because . . .

I'd like to play on a beach because . . .

A "best-fit" solution

Please can I go to tennis – and gym – and music?

I'm at work on tennis evenings, so I can't drive you.

I don't have time to drive you to tennis as well as gym and music.

LET'S SEE WHAT ALTERNATIVES THERE ARE

I want to go to gym and music, but I don't want to go to tennis.

Nobody has time to drive Jo
Sometimes consensus leads to a "best fit" solution, as we hope this will be. Elaine drives Chris and Jo to gym and music lessons during the week. Now Jo would like to start playing tennis, which would mean another car trip. Elaine is not happy about this. Elaine explains that she is too busy to fit in any more driving and Frank says he cannot come home early to take him. Jo is keen to play indoor tennis because she loves it and the school lessons aren't long enough. When each person has explained their point of view, the problem is shared. Perhaps they can draw a "What if" webchart (see below) to generate solutions to the problem.

The challenge here is to think creatively around the problem to find the best solution for everyone.

"WHAT IF" WEBCHART

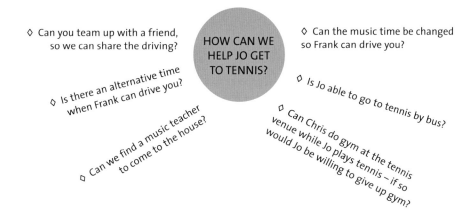

◊ Can you team up with a friend, so we can share the driving?

HOW CAN WE HELP JO GET TO TENNIS?

◊ Can the music time be changed so Frank can drive you?

◊ Is there an alternative time when Frank can drive you?

◊ Can we find a music teacher to come to the house?

◊ Is Jo able to go to tennis by bus?

◊ Can Chris do gym at the tennis venue while Jo plays tennis – if so would Jo be willing to give up gym?

Mediation

> The aim of mediation is to help people end a quarrel amicably by finding common understanding.

Mediation is a similar process to consensus, but it is most often used when there is conflict or a high level of disagreement between two or three people or two or three groups of people. This can be an extremely useful technique with an ongoing problem or one that crops up time after time. The aim is to help people end a quarrel amicably by finding common understanding. The mediator must not take sides because this person has to remain impartial for the process to work successfully. The mediator needs the respect of everyone concerned as well as some understanding of the situation.

Being a mediator is different from the role taken by a facilitator because mediators need to be detached and see all parties to the dispute as being equal, regardless of their own point of view.

You can compare the two processes and decide which is more useful in any given situation.

Good times to use mediation

◊ When there are frequent arguments over the use of a room.
◊ To solve family quarrels about "sharing" or "borrowing" possessions.
◊ When there are disagreements about noisy music.
◊ To solve disputes over spending money.

Solving a long-term family problem
Clare and Sarah are constantly quarrelling about which of their possessions belongs to whom. Start with facts and feelings. As a parent, explain what you see and how you feel about it. Ask them to do the same. Play back a summary so that they know they are understood. This process will help them to calm things down.

Now you can look for common ground and common needs. Perhaps you can agree that some things are special and are not for sharing, while other things are all right to share. They could have a special place or container with their names on it for their own things. Whatever you all decide, the mediator will need to check that the agreement is kept. That way you will build up trust for the future and, with luck, you will solve the problem completely.

> It is important that the disputants work on the problem together and that the decision is not imposed on them.

Stages of mediation

Here is an example of the stages of mediation, which you can adapt as you wish. For most family situations these may be too formal, but the general idea is useful.

Step 1. Start by talking to the disputants separately to see if you can understand their views.

Step 2. When you all meet, agree ground rules (no put-downs, no interruptions, and so on).

Step 3. Allow each person to explain the problem and how they see it, how they feel about it, and what they want to happen. Use "I" statements and the feelings and needs diagram (see pp. 62 and 67).

Step 4. Ask questions and summarize what you have heard. If you get it wrong, give the person a chance to explain again, so that everyone is clear.

Step 5. Summarize the problem in a way that they can each agree with. If there are several issues, start with the easiest.

Step 6. See if people can find common needs or common ground. Is there something they both, or all, want in this situation?

Step 7. Ask people if they have any solutions that meet everyone's needs – and offer some yourself. If there seems to be no acceptable solution, you may need to stop there and try again later.

Step 8. When you have something acceptable, seal the agreement with a promise or contract.

You can adapt the mediation process for solving a whole range of problems, from everyday family issues to complex political ones.

As mediator you need to be even-handed and as objective as you can be. It is very important that you hold the circle and encourage each person to share their feelings, without being aggressive or getting upset.

Bully

Nobody likes me.

I hate everyone.

I want ...!

Victim

I'm no good!

He doesn't like me.

Oh dear!

Bullies and victims

It's not much fun being either a bully or a victim. Our hearts may go out to the victim, but the child who regularly bullies also has problems. A child who bullies as a habit is likely to find he does not make friends easily, while a child who takes on a victim mentality is likely to feel vulnerable and be easily upset.

It's best to avoid labelling a person as a "bully" or as a "victim", even when they seem to behave like that all the time. Once a person becomes labelled the pattern is reinforced, because there is then an expectation that they will always do it. If we stop to notice, we see that most of us find ourselves adopting bully or victim behaviour at some time or the other. It is all a matter of degree.

The problem may be occasional, or low-level, constant, and irritating. Or it may be very distressing. In each case the issues are the same. It won't help if you, or anyone else, comes in on the side of the child who is playing the victim. As the knight in shining armour rushing in to attack the bully and save the victim you are maintaining the pattern. Being a "rescuer" or protector gives the victim lots of encouragement to stay in that role – and you may, yourself, land up being a bully or even a victim, too.

The result is a power triangle, with the victim, bully, and rescuer all feeling stuck and fed up.

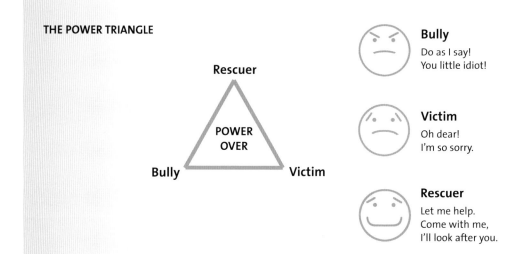

THE POWER TRIANGLE

Rescuer

POWER OVER

Bully   Victim

Bully
Do as I say!
You little idiot!

Victim
Oh dear!
I'm so sorry.

Rescuer
Let me help.
Come with me,
I'll look after you.

Getting out of the impasse

Bullying can work only where there is a victim. If a child tries to push someone around, he will succeed only if the other person accepts it or gets upset by it. When we stand up to bullying or ignore it, bullying does not pay off.

As an adult, it's a help to see yourself in the role of a "mediator" – being strong, calm, and clear at all times. As a mediator, your aim is to shift the balance of power so that it is more equal. In your mind, separate the children from their behaviour so that you can remind yourself of their better qualities. Use the facts, feelings, and needs iceberg diagram (see p. 67) as a guide for this.

Martyr role

Sometimes victims play the more subtle role of the martyr. This is more insidious because the victim does not complain outright. Instead a martyr stores up resentment or secretly thinks they are being heroic when, in fact, they think everything is deeply unfair. If you think a child is being a martyr, you can still come in as the mediator by asking them both how they are feeling.

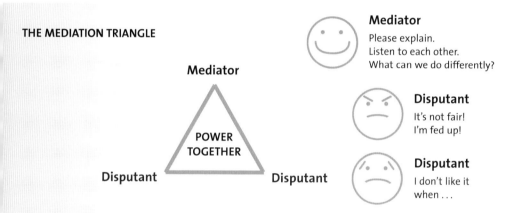

THE MEDIATION TRIANGLE

Mediator

POWER TOGETHER

Disputant   Disputant

Mediator
Please explain.
Listen to each other.
What can we do differently?

Disputant
It's not fair!
I'm fed up!

Disputant
I don't like it when . . .

WHAT YOU CAN DO AS A MEDIATOR

◊ Make contact. Go to the children and speak to them as equals, without taking sides.

◊ Explain to them that you are sad to see them unhappy.

◊ Ask each one to describe the facts as they see them – their feelings and what they would like to happen. (If this is a regular occurrence, make sure you do not ask the same child to speak first each time.)

◊ When you can, you need to affirm both children so they can develop more self-esteem and confidence to be who they really are.

◊ Look for a solution with the children. How you do this will depend on their age and communication skills.

> Bullying can work only where there is a victim.

Moving the situation forward

Sometimes we have problems seeing things from someone else's point of view – a child's, for example, or our partner's. Perhaps we just cannot understand the way they do things or understand their explanations of their behaviour. Perhaps we are always surprised by their response to us.

One way to move the situation forward is to spend time on our own, imagining what it is like to be in the other person's position, so that we can think carefully about them, their experiences, their feelings, and their needs. When we feel we understand them better, we should be able to identify with them to some extent and so appreciate what they are saying. This does not mean that we will necessarily agree with them. If we find this exercise difficult it may be that we need to know more about them or to listen to them more closely.

> The aim is to connect with our own feelings and perspective and then with the feelings and perspective of the other person.

STEPPING IN EACH OTHER'S SHOES

◊ Mark out a place in the room for three different positions. The 1st position is yourself, the 2nd is the missing person, and the 3rd is the bird's eye overview. You may want to have three chairs or you may prefer to stand.

◊ Stand or sit in each position in turn.

◊ Starting in 1st position, connect with your feelings and give yourself a moment to reflect on why you want to do this exercise. Ask yourself what the facts are as you see them. How do you feel? What outcome do you want? You may wish to write the answers down.

◊ Move to the 2nd position, imagining yourself as the other person, and see if you can sit or stand as that person would. Visualize what they look like and imitate their body language so

that you can start to empathize. Now ask yourself the same questions: What are the facts as you see them? How do you feel? What outcome do you want? Try to do this as though you are that person, so that you really start to feel what it is like being them. Again, you may wish to write the answers down.

◊ Now move to the 3rd position, imagining yourself as an outsider, and see if you can find common feelings and needs.

◊ Finish by thanking yourself and the other person, so that you mark the end of the exercise. You may wish to write down some reflections, as yourself.

◊ Please be careful how you do this with a child. You may find there are lots of difficult feelings to be dealt with sympathetically.

This exercise is a role play we can do on our own to help us think more empathetically and creatively about someone we find difficult. The aim is to connect with our own feelings and perspective and then with the feelings and perspective of the other person.

What are the facts? **1st position:**

How do I feel? **Yourself**

What outcome do I want?

What feelings and needs do they have in common?

2nd position:
Other person

What are the facts?

How does he feel?

What outcome would he like?

3rd position:
Overview

Can you think of situations from your own experience when your parents refused to allow you to do something you longed to do?

Were you frustrated or accepting – or did you go ahead and do it anyway?

This can be a time when the family rules keep changing as parents try to understand and deal with these longings to be adventurous.

Security and freedom

One of the most important tasks for any parent is dealing with children's need for experiment and adventure. The urge to explore, risk, test, and challenge is natural and important. It is an intrinsic part of growing up. Children need to become independent and capable of being on their own, to stretch out, channel their energies into exciting new avenues, and gain new experience.

This can be a huge source of conflict. As parents, we often feel that our child wants more freedom than is good for him, that he is testing us, that he is never satisfied or always demanding. Yet he does need to feel cared for and supported, to have a sense of belonging, to have a home where he is always welcome. One minute he is begging to go out, the next he is coming home for reassurance.

There are several reasons why we find it difficult to deal with requests for more freedom.

One is that we do not know how to negotiate new rules and boundaries. Another is that we are worried about the consequences of freedom.

Exploring our fears

Sometimes it can be difficult to let our children go, either because we are fearful or because we think they won't be able to deal with the problems. Yet if we stop them, we are holding them back unnecessarily and they may feel frustrated or even imprisoned.

Fear is one of the biggest obstacles to exploring and risk-taking. Experience teaches us that we cannot trust everyone and that there may be dangers out there. But sometimes our fears are based on rumours or exaggerations. The facts may be distorted by the media or by anxious neighbours. Conflicts between groups can grow and grow simply because people listen to hearsay and opinion instead of going out and making direct contact. This attitude leads to mistrust that grows outward in ever-increasing ripples, from neighbours to communities and from countries to regions.

In city neighbourhoods, disputes may be fuelled by the local media publishing extreme viewpoints in order to get a story. Readers assume the worst and take sides without asking questions or stopping to listen. Fear of the streets may or may not be realistic. But until we get the facts straight, we do not know.

Dealing with fear

At some time or the other, most parents experience the agony of waiting up at night and worrying about their teenage children. Allowing them to go out on their own can be hard. When a child makes a challenging demand on you, the most important thing you need to do is to look carefully at your own feelings and find out the facts, so that you can make an informed and sensible decision. As a child acquires more experience, you will get a clearer sense of what he is able to do and what risks he can take.

Where we live, the shops and buses are only a short walk away, but the route is up a winding, badly lit road. At times I struggled to balance my own fear and our children's need for independence. When they were old enough, I was happy for them to go to the shops, except in the dark. In the winter I used to be very thankful that they could just get home from school before nightfall. Later, when my daughter went out at night, I tried to make sure she went with her friends or, alternatively, we would fetch her home ourselves or encourage her to stay overnight. When she was older, I had to allow her to go alone, but I was always a little nervous. As far as I knew, this dark street was perfectly safe and so I had to get my fear in perspective and let her go.

> The urge to explore, risk, test, and challenge is natural and important. It is an intrinsic part of growing up.

◊ Fear can be good because it can protect and warn us about danger. It can make us hesitate, perhaps draw back or reconsider.

◊ Fear can also make us defensive, so that we either retreat or attack. Fear can turn our houses into castles. It can become a habit – a way of thinking that informs our every action. It can stunt us and make us reluctant to try new challenges.

FEAR CAN TURN OUR HOMES INTO CASTLES

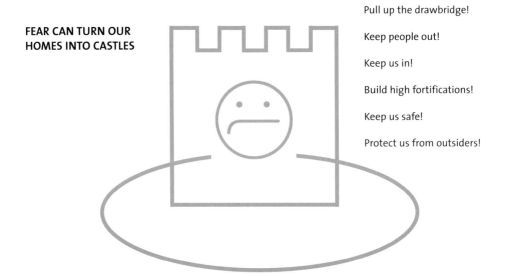

Pull up the drawbridge!

Keep people out!

Keep us in!

Build high fortifications!

Keep us safe!

Protect us from outsiders!

When we are worried or fearful we usually respond in one of three ways:

◊ As a warrior or knight, going out to attack our foes.
◊ As a rescuer or protector, shielding our child.
◊ As an enabler or supporter, helping him to acquire the skills and resources he needs.

RESPONSES TO FEAR

Can you think of times when you have adopted one or other of these responses? One mother watched her 12-year-old go to the bus stop and wait for the bus each morning. She didn't follow him, but every day she watched him through her binoculars. Her fears may have been justified, we don't know. Perhaps she was worried about a particular person who also waited at the stop. Was there something more useful that she could have done about it?

An enabling parent works with his child to build up a realistic picture of the situation and his ability to cope with it.

I'm going to sort them out!
Bring them to justice!

Warrior

Come to me – I'll look after you!
Poor you – I'll deal with this
How awful they are!

Rescuer

How sad. Let's see what we can do about it.
What a pity! What can we/you do about it?
Let's make a plan.

Enabler

GOING ON A JOURNEY
How to deal with security and fear

As a general rule it is good to minimize the risks and maximize the opportunity for a good experience. When your child wants to do something new that you feel is risky, it may help to think about it together, as you would any new journey.

You could:
◊ Find out what the plans are so you have a mental map of what he will be doing.
What is the venue like?
Who else will be there?
How safe is it?
Do some research if you wish, so you have the facts straight.

◊ Think about the skills and information he has.
Is he going with friends and what experience do they have?

◊ Is there anything else he needs, such as a taxi phone number, a street map, spare money?

◊ Does he have contingency plans?

◊ Having talked the plan through, how do you feel about it?
If you are not happy about it, can you think of something that will make it all right?
Perhaps you need to generate some alternatives.

Preparation for a journey
Where are you going?
What will you do there?
Who are you going with?
How will you get there?
What information do you need to help you – a street map, for example?
How are you getting home, and at what time?
What skills/resources do you need – a phone, for example?
What contingency plans do we need to make?
How confident are we?
Is it all right to do this, now?

REMEMBER
◊ Be objective about the likelihood of a problem becoming a reality.

◊ Reflect on your fears.

Ask yourself:

Do your fears seem reasonable?

Is something promoting your fears, such as news items, opinions, and rumours?

Or is your fear justified?

If so, what constructive action are you going to take?

The skills and
attitudes of
peaceable living
that we learn at
home are a
resource for the
rest of our lives,
and the lives of
those we influence.

6 Connecting

Creating a culture of peace

We cannot escape the fact that issues of conflict and peace confront us, no matter which way we turn: in schools, on the streets, in families, between gangs and ethnic or religious groups, and between nations and groups of nations. What is clear is that the underlying patterns of conflict, of competition, bullying, fury, and frustration are repeated over and over again in many situations, wherever people feel angry, threatened, or fearful. Violent behaviour may result from lack of care and understanding in childhood. But equally it may result from injustice and violence inflicted by unfair government policies or by military intervention.

The skills and attitudes of peaceable living that we learn at home are a resource for the rest of our lives, and the lives of those we influence. As we move beyond the family we take these skills and attitudes with us into schools, neighbourhoods, work, and beyond. In many different and important ways we can help to create a more peaceable world.

> In many different and important ways we can help to create a more peaceable world.

There are three broad ways we can help build the culture of peace:

◊ Living according to our values
The skills and ideas we learn are a resource for life, to be copied and developed, as we gain experience. They are like seeds that we can spread in everyday relationships in every area of our lives, in our neighbourhoods, schools, workplaces, local councils, and national campaigns.

◊ Negotiating and mediating in crises
Peaceful negotiation starts from the view that groups can respect and understand one another. When one group has more power than the other and threatens to use it, then the negotiation will neither be equal nor peaceable. However, there is a real opportunity for peace when everyone meets around the table to find common ground.

◊ Campaigning
Effective campaigns need good communicators; people who can win support for their cause. But, again, to do this peacefully they need to be respectful as well as honest and fair.

There is no one route to a more peaceable society. It involves a change in priorities, attitudes, and beliefs among the powerful, including politicians, company directors, shareholders, financiers, and the military. It also requires a change on an everyday level, so that there is a groundswell of public opinion in favour of peace and familiarity with the tools of peace. This grassroots change is often referred to as "creating a culture of peace".

The consequences of inaction

Learning to live together in peace is crucial not only for our immediate needs, but also for the sake of the world. If we do not try to do this, we will eventually destroy life as we know it. In the past, human survival has involved putting ourselves, our family, and perhaps our country first. But ever since we saw the earliest photographs of Earth from space, we have become increasingly aware of the fragility of our planet and our interdependence. With threats from weapons of mass destruction and climate change we are now beginning to see that keeping our focus on ourselves and our country alone will not guarantee our safety.

Our survival must become a shared goal, one in which we learn to live and work together. This involves a huge turnaround in our thinking and attitudes, which it is not impossible to achieve. Once we try to understand and connect to others we start to discover common ground and common needs. Living and working becomes more of a joint venture. It can be done. Whatever we choose to do, we will make a difference. The skills and ideas described in the earlier sections of this book can help you do this. The family is like a seed bed, where we can learn the skills of peaceable living not only to help ourselves, but also to help others.

> Learning to live together in peace is crucial not only for our immediate needs, but also for the sake of the world. If we do not try to do this, we will eventually destroy life as we know it.

> The more a home reflects what is important to us, the more we will appreciate it and enjoy it.

Making a peaceable home

The atmosphere, appearance, and activities in your home can all help to create a peaceable family life. Peace is not only to do with the obvious things, such as keeping the noise levels down and staying calm. Colour and light, the use of space, our possessions, the presence of plants and animals can all make your home more convivial to peaceable living.

In the Western world we are encouraged to acquire and consume so much that we may feel we are on a conveyor belt that constantly pulls us along. However, we also have the choice to stop and question. Feng shui, the ancient Chinese art of placement, is probably the ultimate way to rethink our homes and their contents, but there are several simpler steps that you might wish to take. You might, for example, find it helpful to ask yourself some of the questions below and to pick out some changes you would like to make. Something quite simple and straightforward might be particularly beneficial.

What are the activities that matter to you? Can you do them comfortably? Or would you like to rearrange things?
List the activities that you want to encourage in your family and think creatively about how to bring them about.

CONDUCTING A FAMILY AUDIT

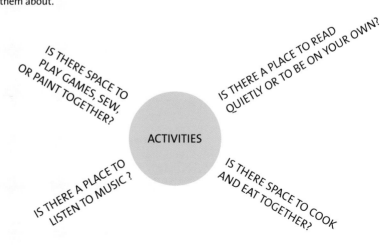

IS THERE SPACE TO PLAY GAMES, SEW, OR PAINT TOGETHER?

IS THERE A PLACE TO READ QUIETLY OR TO BE ON YOUR OWN?

ACTIVITIES

IS THERE A PLACE TO LISTEN TO MUSIC?

IS THERE SPACE TO COOK AND EAT TOGETHER?

Is this a good time to declutter?

Do you have a TV in every room? Or will you choose to restrict them so that they don't start to dominate? Do you really need loads of storage space for all your possessions? Or are you going to limit them so that you can encourage less consumer-orientated activities? Do your possessions reflect your interests and values? Or have you got so much of everything already that you don't need any more? As we have seen, it takes time and energy to become involved in projects and hobbies, and some pursuits need equipment.

How would you like your home to feel?

What is the effect of the colours and lighting? Colour, light, and space can affect our mood. Do the colours in your house reflect the atmosphere you would like to create? Where would you like stimulation and where would you like peace and quiet?

Does your home reflect your wider values?

What people put in their homes reflects their values. Do you have energy-saving light bulbs and equipment and places for recycling? Do you buy organic, fair-traded food? The more a home reflects what is important to us, the more we will appreciate it and enjoy it.

FAMILY DISCUSSION
If you need to make changes, get everyone involved in thinking about one another's needs, both as individuals and as a group. You might have a family discussion where you ask everyone to focus on people's needs and wishes, both as individuals and as caring members of the family.

POSSESSIONS

◊ Have you got things you don't need any more?
◊ Do you have too many unnecessary or distracting electronic gadgets?
◊ Are your possessions relevant to the things you enjoy doing?

ATMOSPHERE

◊ Are there places to be quiet?
◊ Are there places to be together?
◊ Does your home feel welcoming?

VALUES

◊ Do you recycle and save energy?
◊ Is your home a reflection of what matters to you?
◊ Do you buy fair-traded or organic products?

> When you feel isolated or going against the tide, it helps to have a supportive group to turn to. You can express your worries and your hopes freely . . .

Home from home

On our peace path, it helps to have companions who have similar ideas and beliefs, with whom we can share problems and solutions. In a supportive, caring group of this kind, adults and children alike can gain confidence, learn new peace-making skills, and widen their circle of experience and understanding. This is a community where everyone can feel truly "at home". For children it can be an important stepping stone as they move away from the family.

Such a group may be a sports club or gym, where there are team activities and a common space. It could be a faith group that welcomes families, or a local group such as the Guides or Scouts. Or it could be a babysitting circle or a group of neighbours. Such a group might start with parents coming together and grow to include everyone – children and perhaps "aunts" and "uncles", too. Whichever kind of group you have, it is important that there is a balance between caring for everyone and also being open-minded toward other people and other groups.

One of the best things about a group of like-minded people is that within it you have shared values. When you feel isolated or you are swimming against the tide, you have a supportive group to turn to. You can express your worries and your hopes, knowing that you will be heard with respect and understanding. This need not be a formal group. It can be a small self-created group that evolves among friends.

For example, a group of neighbours where we live formed a small baby-sitting circle and started to have parties for all the members to get to know each other. Some of them went on holiday together and quickly built strong friendships, which, thirty years later, are as strong as ever. Today, those children are going to one another's weddings and although they are now scattered, they seem set to stay in touch.

Creating your own group

To create your own group, it may be easiest to aim at a relatively small one of about four or five families. You can get to know each other, so that relationships become strong and caring – more like aunts, uncles, and cousins. Perhaps adults will share their particular interests with one another and meet together in support or listening groups. They may take each other's children out on trips or teach them their skills. Shared activities of any type give everyone a chance to develop caring relationships and learn the skills of living together.

A home from home is one where everyone can:

◊ Feel supported, trusted, appreciated, and valued.
◊ Discuss issues that trouble them and generate solutions.
◊ Use their peace-making skills and spread their ideas.
◊ Enjoy activities together.
◊ Feel they have a role or a purpose.

Please remember that in order to build peace, it is also important to connect with others. Faith groups may look for ecumenical or interfaith activities, sports teams can play against teams from other areas, and groups of neighbours can visit other places.

The benefit of such a group is that it can help us to live the way we want to live. It can support us on our peace journey and help us to become the kind of family we choose to be.

> The virtual reality of the screen can replace the reality of our own everyday experience and relationships.

TV and computers

Television and computers may widen our horizons by extending our knowledge and opening our eyes to people and places outside our immediate experience. But how does this knowledge and experience help us to become more peaceable? Studies suggest that too much screen watching is bad for our physical and emotional health. The more time we – adults and children – spend watching TV or playing computer games, the less time we spend on other activities, such as talking to one another, taking up hobbies and exercise, or going out. The virtual reality of the screen can replace the reality of our own everyday experience and relationships. Specifically the more time we spend watching violence the more immune to it we become, and the harder it becomes for us to distinguish clearly between fact and fiction.

To find out how TV and computers affect your child, the best thing you can do is to watch with her and see how she responds to it. Ask yourself:

What are the messages she is picking up? Television can be entertaining and enriching. It can also be boring and blunt the senses. Violence is only part of the picture. Look at the message behind the story. Does it demonstrate real-life issues in a constructive, caring way? Or does it promote an aggressive, acquisitive, and competitive lifestyle? Are the heroes and heroines polite and caring or are they angry and greedy? How are sex and love portrayed?

What is her response? Some children's television programmes are designed to involve the viewer by setting them puzzles and asking questions. However, most programmes require no response and so you may find that your child is half watching, half dozing. This is not usually the best way either to relax or to engage with something. Over time, there is a "drip-drip" effect of seeing a lot of violence on the screen, even in a state of half-awareness. Violence becomes less shocking and more acceptable. Computer games require more participation, but they can be addictive. Watch how your child is engaged. Is she obsessive and mesmerized, or is she having fun and learning?

What you can do about screen watching

◊ Aim for a balance so that your child can enjoy watching and learning from TV and computers.

◊ Decide together what she is allowed to watch. Sometimes watch with her and encourage her to talk about what she sees.

◊ Agree a time limit.

◊ Limit the number of TVs and computers in your home and consider their location. As far as possible, have them in communal areas so that watching TV or using a computer does not become a solitary activity, but is one that is at least partly shared.

◊ Watch DVDs that convey messages compatible with your own values.

◊ Find books and audio tapes that convey knowledge in different ways and stimulate your child's imagination.

◊ Discuss these issues in family get-togethers.

WATCHING TV – THE MESSAGE FROM THE SCREEN

How much violence is there?

What kind of attitudes does it promote?

How are the heroes and heroines portrayed?

Does it demonstrate real-life issues in a constructive way?

TV RULES
◊ Average maximum time per day – 1½ hours.
◊ Discuss which programmes to watch.
◊ Choose some programmes to watch together.
◊ Find time to talk about what you've watched.

Choosing a peaceable school

When deciding on which pre-schools and schools to send your children to, it is worth visiting all of the ones on your shortlist so that you can get a feel for them, meet the teaching staff, and see what facilities they have and how the students appear to respond to each other, the teaching staff, and the environment. In many cases, our first impressions, or gut reactions, are accurate, so we should take note of them.

To choose the right school for your child, one with a peaceable environment, look around and ask relevant questions. Watch the children as well as the teachers. Do the teachers and carers encourage the children to respect one another and to take responsibility? In general, are the children:

◊ **Comfortable** with themselves?
◊ **Caring** of one another?
◊ **Communicating** well among themselves and with the teaching staff?
◊ **Capable** of solving problems constructively?

You could also use these headings as a checklist when choosing a carer or minder.

Teachers whose aim it is to create a peaceable environment will use a positive teaching style that includes discussion about problems and boundaries. In this way, children will have a framework that they understand and within which they can work. The teacher will also encourage children to take responsibility for their actions and show them what they can do if they are angry.

A PEACEABLE CLASSROOM

Here are 10 signs of a peaceable classroom to look out for:

1. A peaceable school will encourage parents to come in to talk or help with outings, special projects, or listening to individual children reading. If there is a problem of some sort, the teacher will find time to help sort it out.

2. Most children can easily be taught to Stop and Think before they hurt someone or shout out. If you are able to watch the class, you may be able to see whether the teacher encourages this.

3. Reparation is preferable to punishment, so look to see if the teacher encourages a child to tidy up a mess that she has made or help someone she has hurt.

4. Find out what the school does to discourage bullying. Some have counsellors or give counselling training to teachers. Cooperative activities help to create an inclusive atmosphere.

5. One of the most common routines in a peaceable classroom is the "Circle Time", when the teacher and children can talk things over together. They may talk about the classroom rules so that everyone can understand them and take some responsibility for keeping to them.

6. They will also discuss what happens when pupils break the rules, so that they are clear about the consequences of disobedience.

7. You might wish to ask the teacher how they discipline the children. A procedure that is open and clear will mean that each child knows what will happen if the rules are broken.

8. Older children may learn skills, such as peer mediation, so that they can solve problems constructively for themselves.

9. Ask how the school celebrates the festivals of different cultures and faiths. Participation in these may seem superficial, but it will help pupils to respect and understand other cultures and religions and all those who may be different from themselves.

10. In the curriculum, look for topics such as caring for one another and learning about other people. Some teachers encourage empathy by using role play, so that children can begin to identify with each other.

Dealing with bullying

In many countries, school authorities and individual schools have anti-bullying policies and measures to prevent bullying are on the curriculum. Teachers may use role play so that children can find out what it is like to both be a victim and a bully. They can also use techniques of role play to learn about mediation (see pp. 108–9). Some schools train older children in peer mediation so that problems, such as bullying, are seen as a group responsibility to deal with.

When you visit a school you can enquire about the procedures that are in place to deal with specific problems. Some schools have a post box where pupils can post anonymous letters indicating the class they are in. Class teachers will then be asked to follow this matter up by talking generally about bullying and observing what is happening in the class or classes

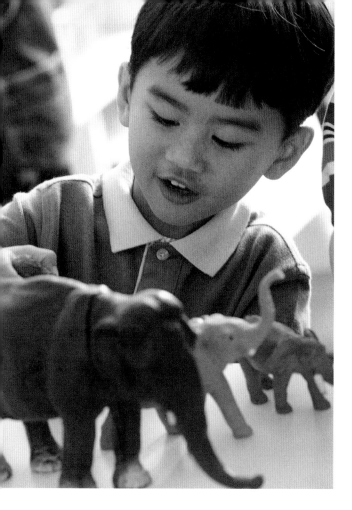

concerned. In some schools, one member of staff will be a trained play therapist or counsellor, who will be available to deal with these and other issues. Some organize a break-time drop-in centre, where children can go to talk to them about whatever it is concerning or worrying them. In some other schools, the catering staff might be trained to encourage constructive play among the children and to watch out for inappropriate behaviour, such as bullying.

In some inner-city environments where violent crime is a problem, peace organizations plan and conduct road shows with workshops on the dangers of drugs, carrying weapons, gangs, and bullying.

If you or your child is worried about bullying, you must feel able to take your concern to the school and have your concerns taken seriously. (For more on bullying see pp. 110–11.)

Getting involved in the local community

Building the culture of peace will take us beyond family, friends, and school to include our neighbourhoods and towns. Getting involved in your local community is one way you can extend the culture of peace. You may like to use your peacemaking skills in neighbourhood mediation or campaigning for a safer environment. Or you may choose activities that simply widen your circle of friends and acquaintances, and in this way give yourself a stronger sense of community. You might like to do something that involves children and young people, or you might decide that the first step is to get involved yourself, without them.

Most of us have quite a few possible choices, so why not make a webchart of them to clarify your thinking (see also pp. 96–9)?

CHOICES WEBCHART

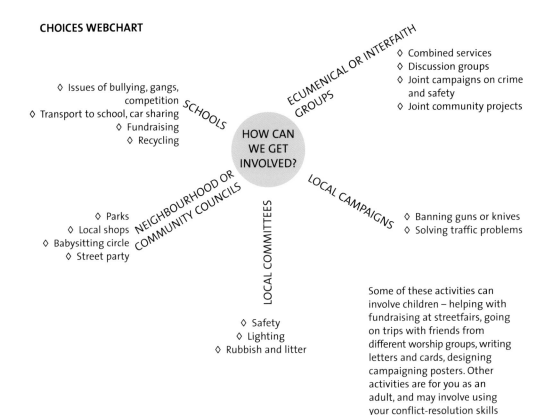

SCHOOLS
◊ Issues of bullying, gangs, competition
◊ Transport to school, car sharing
◊ Fundraising
◊ Recycling

ECUMENICAL OR INTERFAITH GROUPS
◊ Combined services
◊ Discussion groups
◊ Joint campaigns on crime and safety
◊ Joint community projects

HOW CAN WE GET INVOLVED?

NEIGHBOURHOOD OR COMMUNITY COUNCILS
◊ Parks
◊ Local shops
◊ Babysitting circle
◊ Street party

LOCAL CAMPAIGNS
◊ Banning guns or knives
◊ Solving traffic problems

LOCAL COMMITTEES
◊ Safety
◊ Lighting
◊ Rubbish and litter

Some of these activities can involve children – helping with fundraising at streetfairs, going on trips with friends from different worship groups, writing letters and cards, designing campaigning posters. Other activities are for you as an adult, and may involve using your conflict-resolution skills with other adults.

Taking back our community

Developing a sense of community begins in our streets and neighbourhoods, so that we feel safe and comfortable enough to visit one another freely. The more people walk around their neighbourhood, the more they get a sense of what is going on, the safer they feel, and the more contact they have with one another. One way to promote contact with your neighbours is to organize street activities. In several countries there are organizations, such as Safer Streets and Living Streets, that focus on the street as a safe and friendly meeting place, where people can come together to create neighbourhood communities. You may be able to obtain information from them or you can just go ahead and make your own plans.

Getting involved in your local community is one way you can extend the culture of peace.

Street activities for all the family could include:

◊ Holding street parties, where you are granted permission to close the street off to traffic for a few hours so that you can have an open-air party.

◊ Planting trees and flowers to make the streets more attractive and having things that people can care for as a joint project.

◊ Campaigning to reduce the speed and flow of traffic to make streets safer, perhaps so that children can play out together.

◊ Supporting your traditional corner shop – if you still have one.

> To create peace, we cannot build walls around ourselves; instead we must find ways to build bridges.

Making connections

To build peace we need support from those we feel comfortable with and we also need to reach out to others. It can be rather more challenging to connect with those whom we do not understand and perhaps fear. But if we are serious about peace, this is something we need to think about. To create peace, we cannot build walls around ourselves; instead we must find ways to build bridges.

BRIDGES, NOT WALLS

We need building blocks – such as family and neighbourhood support, respect for self and others, sharing, listening, communication skills, and self-confidence – in order to reach out and bridge the gap to connect with others.

Empathy · Caring · Listening · Connection · Sharing · Respect · Support and skills · Confidence

The ideas and tools in this book are intended to provide a resource for building bridges, not walls. As we learn to be comfortable with ourselves and caring of others, we may find bridges come naturally. The more we listen to others, the more we discover that we all have similar basic needs and fears. We have the same longings for security, safety, sympathy, and support, though we find them in different ways.

There are many things we can do to build bridges in our community. Some of these may involve children directly, while others may be activities we engage in on behalf of everyone of all ages.

WAYS TO BUILD BRIDGES

School exchanges

Some schools twin with schools in a different area or country. They arrange exchanges so that groups of pupils get to visit for a day or a week, say, discovering what it is like to be in a different environment. Afterwards, they may engage in a shared project or keep up group correspondence. In some cases, schools of different faiths exchange students so that they can learn about other people's religions and beliefs.

Faith groups

Some temples, churches, mosques, and synagogues participate in joint activities. To help us build bridges we need to recognize that all the world's major faiths share fundamental, common beliefs. Sadly, sometimes these beliefs are half hidden by rituals and writings that separate them. Many groups, of all faiths, believe that only they have found the one, true way to God and do not see that there may be other paths to the same place of love and compassion. However, when we look at different faiths, we see, for example, that Hindus speak about the importance of Seva, which is giving service to the community voluntarily; Jews emphasize the responsibility of sharing with one another and promoting justice and peace; Mohammed spoke specifically about becoming close to God and caring for one another, particularly for the sick and the poor; Christ taught that we should examine ourselves and find fault with others only if we are without fault ourselves. Interfaith groups know from experience that when people make contact, their rituals are no longer barriers to divide, but opportunities to share.

Local councils

Most towns and cities are made up of a diverse range of communities. When you become involved locally in your school or community, you are not only helping others, you are also demonstrating to your children the importance of participation and involvement. One way to get involved with different groups is to participate in local councils, either as an elected representative or as a community volunteer. In many cities, local councils organize community fairs, where different groups have their own stalls and perform dance and music. Just going along on the day is a great way to have fun and learn about the community you and your family live in.

THE OLD WATERWORKS
Case study

In many countries, major developments require community consultation. In one recent case in Britain, an old water-purification plant, which had been disused for years, became a topic for discussion. The council wanted to build housing and a hypermarket on the site. Local shopkeepers feared that they would lose trade and be forced to close. Local residents were keen on having a store, but were worried that the plans did not include any schools – which would mean overcrowding in the existing ones. Local environmentalists saw there was to be a large car park and feared the streets would be jammed with extra traffic.

All the groups had their own ideas and the arguments were fierce, but in the end they came to a compromise, which the council agreed to. The new store was scaled down to a supermarket, the car park was to be made smaller, and a new school was also to be built on the site.

When people sit down together to listen and negotiate respectfully, many problems can be peaceably resolved – just as they were in this case study. Why not use your peace-making skills to get involved in similar activities?

> One of the most important messages we can give to our children, and to others, is that there are alternatives to war. Another way is possible.

Promoting a peaceable agenda

Most people say that they want peace, but many think they can win that objective through war. They believe that violence can clear the air so that people are ready for peace. But war sets up barriers between people so that they no longer see one another as human beings, as people like themselves. Eventually one side might become so ground down that they beg for peace, but the damage done can take generations to recover from.

Violence breeds violence

For example, people generally believed that the 1914–18 war in Europe would be the "war to end all wars". Little did they suspect that after hundreds of thousands of soldiers had died in the trenches only twenty-one years would elapse before another war in the same place would occur. The belief that wars can bring peace is a myth – violence always creates more violence. For a time, one side may be cowed into submission, but this is not true peace. It is simply a type of schoolyard bullying, in which the stronger kid beats up the weaker one.

To stop the vicious circle of violence we have to take positive, peaceful action. Now! One of the most important messages we can give to our children, and to others, is that there are alternatives to war. Another way is possible.

All the peace-making skills and attitudes that we can use with our families and friends are equally applicable in a wider, world context. Skills such as mediation, consensus decision-making, problem-solving, and listening and expressing our feelings can all be applied wherever we go. In New Zealand, for example, mediation has become an integral part of solving community and inter-personal disputes. In the countries of the former Yugoslavia, reconciliation is coming about through what are known as "listening groups", in which people from different sides and ethnic backgrounds share what they went through during the war.

There are lots of things we can do to support peace in the world. Here are some examples:

SUPPORTING CONSTRUCTIVE CAMPAIGNS AGAINST WEAPONS

Weapons are a major problem, not only in Western cities, but also in regional conflicts all around the world. Locally, you may be able to support community projects that lobby for controls on guns and knives and teach people how to survive without them. On a global level, you can join campaigns against the trade in arms.

Of course, we will always be able to hurt one another with any weapon that comes to hand, whether it is a rock or a pocket knife. Guns, however, come into a different category because they can be used so easily and impersonally, without immediate direct contact or engagement. Like knives, there is a certain glamour attached to guns that makes them especially attractive to a certain type of person. If you are concerned about this problem in your immediate area, you should find out more about organizations such as the Peace Alliance, which operates in several UK cities.

LINKING WITH PEACE-BUILDING PROJECTS ABROAD

Many international charities or faith groups support peace organizations in countries where violence is common. Some of these have "link projects", which put groups in Western countries in touch with those in war-torn regions. You can involve children in a variety of activities, such as learning about the people, fund-raising, and writing letters.

My local peace group is planning to give support to an inter-faith school for Moslems, Jews, and Christians in Israel-Palestine. From experience in Northern Ireland and elsewhere, it is clear that whereas segregated schools tend to promote division, hatred, and fear, schools that are integrated can lay the foundations for a new generation of understanding. This particular school, in Ramallah, is a beacon for trust-building and mutual cooperation and we hope that our support will be useful to them in some small way. We also hope that we – adults and children alike – will learn from them and tell others about them.

CONSTRUCTIVE PROTEST

Protests can be effective when they speak to people's hearts, gather support, and lead to talking.

If you wish to protest against war and violence, find ways to make a constructive statement. Hold prayers or light candles in your windows; decorate fences with flowers; explain your message; hand out leaflets; have a peace stall at a local event; collect and take a sack of letters to your local political representatives and ask to meet them; or arrange a public meeting with a speaker to talk about peace-building initiatives.

I know of several peace groups that involve children and teenagers in campaigns. For example, when we were campaigning against the Iraq war, we organized a special peace event for all ages at one of the city art galleries. The young people also helped to make posters for peace vigils and wrote letters to our member of parliament.

STORIES OF PEACEMAKING

Many newspapers give a one-sided version of a story, routinely showing the worst in one group and the best in another. For example, there has been little in our media about the peace movement in either Iraq or Afghanistan. Yet in both countries there have been peaceful demonstrations and prayers for peace, some of which have been interrupted by foreign soldiers firing on them because they were frightened of the crowds.

Some people go into war-torn areas to make a personal stand for peace, such as the ecumenical peace observers who go to Israel-Palestine to accompany people trying peacefully to get on with their everyday lives. The peace observers go with them past blockades and support them when they ask for their rights. Their presence usually stops soldiers firing, though there have been sad cases of observers themselves being killed.

Many people who have suffered most from war and violence find in their hearts the capacity to offer compassion and connection to those who hurt them. In their actions we can find inspiration.

We need to tell each other, especially our children, the types of stories shown here as we work together to build peace. They show that people can stand for peace even in the midst of war. They demonstrate the power of forgiveness and nonviolence to transform people and communities.

Encouraged by the words of the bishop of New York, Reverend Mark Sisk, one New York parish raised enough money to rebuild a mosque in Kabul, Afghanistan, that had been destroyed by American bombing. The two disparate communities are now in regular contact with one another.

In Israel, a Jewish man whose daughter was killed by Palestinians has founded the Parents' Circle, which brings together bereaved parents from both communities. In a ten-month period in 2002–3, more than 200,000 people spoke to one another on the phone about their sorrow.

After the September 11 attack on New York and Washington in 2001, families who lost loved ones formed a group called Peaceful Tomorrows to seek non-violent responses to terrorism.

A British Iraqi has returned to Iraq to set up a liaison centre in which people come to tell their story and seek redress. Many people in Iraq have weapons, but using them rarely provides constructive solutions to problems. "I have to reach people," he says, "before they pick up their guns again."

When the French were testing nuclear weapons in the South Pacific, many people in Australia responded by boycotting French goods. A group of women decided to do something more constructive and different, so they ran a French-style café in the streets and talked to passers-by about the issues.

We have seen that in any conflict there are three basic choices:

Fight: To follow the way of violence in which fear, hurt, and anger lead us to construct walls and barriers between people.

Flight: To keep out of the way.

Turnaround: To follow the way of nonviolence in which connection, empathy, and partnership help us to build bridges toward each other.

Most of us know what each of these choices feels like because, at some time or another, we have all responded in each of these ways. Sometimes it seemed as though we had no choice, and perhaps it was almost true. At other times we saw several choices and we chose to build a bridge.

When we find ourselves in the spiral of violence we become hooked into an increasingly intensive relationship generating anger and fear. We become more and more frightened of others, unable to see alternative ways to behave, utterly defensive, and locked into a destructive pattern. However, when we unwind that spiral we look outward. We ask questions and create alternatives. We reach out and connect. We find common ground and common needs.

The challenge of peaceable parenting is to help our family take the peaceable path. Bridge-building is essential wherever we are and whatever we are doing. The same values of respect, understanding, equality, honesty, compassion, and cooperation are needed to build the pillars of the bridge, and the same tools of negotiation, consensus, and reconciliation are needed to help us cross it. Whether we are at home or at work, among our family or neighbours, in the classroom or the playground, in court or council chamber, all these values and tools can help to create a culture of peace.

I hope that this book will help you to take the peaceable path as often as you can.

> The challenge of peaceable parenting is to help our family take the peaceable path. Bridge-building is essential wherever we are and whatever we are doing.

Index

Author's acknowledgements
My thanks to family and friends, especially Helena Beddoe, Joanna Godfrey Wood and Yvonne Fuchs, as well as to the Quaker project Turning the Tide. I would also like to thank Leap, Confronting Conflict for allowing me to use the Power Triangle and the Icebergs.

Photographic credits
GETTY IMAGES:
Annie Griffiths Belt, 2-3; Gordon Wiltsie, 5; Andre Peristein, 7; Terry Husebye, 11; Judith Haeusler, 25; Philip & Karen Smith, 31; Stockdisc, 38 ; Roy Gumpel, 49; SW Productions, 53; Nick Daly, 73; Peter Poulides, 81; Buccina Studios, 91; Jan Tove Johansson, 113; Peter Cade, 119; Andreanna Seymore, 128; Photodisc Collection 130–1.

Neil White, 13;
Steve Teague, 20, 59, 61, 64;
Bubbles Photo Library/Lois Joy Thurston p89;
Mandy Bell, 125.